VOLUME 22   NUMBER 4   2016

The Child Now

Edited by Julian Gill-Peterson, Rebekah Sheldon,
and Kathryn Bond Stockton

INTRODUCTION

What Is the Now, Even of Then?

**Julian Gill-Peterson, Rebekah Sheldon,
and Kathryn Bond Stockton**

What are we to make of the unexpected future in which we find ourselves? With this open question, we framed "Child Matters," a conference hosted by Indiana University in 2015, in celebration of the recent efflorescence of work in childhood studies. Across the twentieth century, of course, the child and the future circled each other with close reciprocity. Planning and conducting this conference, however, we came to realize that the *concept* of the future has changed in *this* century. In this age of potential extinctions, the question of the future is no longer primarily social or even exclusively human; in the catastrophe of climate change, the future can no longer be counted on to serve as a blank backdrop for human life. It asks us, instead, to reckon with new forms of temporal change. Will plastic objects "outlive" Time, if human time expires? Increasingly, the drama of the plastic water bottle projects its own futurities. Chronology falters. Time grows stranger.

The child, to be sure, has been a creature of chronology. Built on the assembly lines of the last one hundred years, the child now stands for a future out-of-date. Therefore, we propose that the study of the child find new concepts. The task of recalibrating our theoretical instruments and object relations is one that we undertake in this special issue. We offer the now not as a displacement or dismissal of the future but as a mutation of our attention: toward the unique strangeness of childhood as of today. Indeed, the most striking dimension of the "now" that titles this issue is that it has been anything but static or rooted in a stable present. When we first conceived of this issue almost three years ago, the gay child still felt oddly new, and the transgender child still ghostly. The utter disregard for refugee and undocumented children and the killings of African American children by police were not new phenomena—both have long and complex histories—but it was not a certainty these children would soon occupy such a central place in

GLQ 22:4

DOI 10.1215/10642684-3603078

© 2016 by Duke University Press

battles over definitions of the local and the global, the national and the international. Some question of the future inheres for all these children, but something else about their irruptive force inside the "now" commanded our attention a few years ago, as it does today. The children of the twenty-first century are making what counts as the now move ever more quickly, without much time for us to catch our breath. Through their play in the remains of rapidly obsolescing narratives, the figures of children we've collected in this volume deform what we thought we knew about the past as they forge new modes of speculation in the present.

Perhaps oddly, then, thinking the child *now* also means to move orthogonally from an emphasis on futurity to an interest in the historicity of the present. Here queer studies might engage more robustly with the fields of children's literature, childhood studies, and the history of childhood. Anglo-American childhood studies has investigated the production of modern childhood as a form of idealized shelter meant to grow the gap between a person's birth and their adulthood. By taking children in the Progressive Era off the streets, out of factories, and placing them into mass schooling or institutions for juvenile delinquency, childhood was constituted as an ostensibly empty innocence based in deferral and delay: of work, of sex, and of civil rights.[1] Children were then assigned the vital task of directing our consumption, of leading the economy toward a fully consumer mode of demographics and leisure. This childhood for the twentieth century was deeply, doggedly gendered, with the meanings of innocence for boys and girls shoring up the boundaries of domesticity and the desired, but difficult to induce, heterosexuality that was supposed to be childhood's end. As early as 1970, Shulamith Firestone had identified the innocent child as the thin scrim of ideology covering the multiplex effects of dependency. Childhood, for Firestone, is just another name for heteropatriarchy. Robin Bernstein's *Racial Innocence* (2011) crucially adds that American childhood also hoarded innocence to make modern childhood the exclusive property of (propertied) whiteness, with tragic effects. While immigrant children from Europe were forcibly whitened in the new public schools and settlement houses of major cities, African American youth were dispossessed of the status of childhood altogether and made available for imprisonment and exploitation by the withholding of innocence.

While these narratives remain in force, the twenty-first century has also witnessed massive breakdowns in the fantasized modernity of US childhood. Child labor was never eradicated by Progressive reforms, but merely reorganized and made less visible. Today, the notion that childhood offers a wondrous shelter from work feels, finally, unconvincing. The longer children wait to work, the higher their future debt as adults. In the meantime, public education lies in the grip of collapse after decades of planned state disinvestment and public education's failure to pursue seriously the project of racial integration. The employment prospects of many children seem bleak, given that wages have proved mostly stagnant in this century, despite most workers' increased productivity and longer hours. Credit card debt, student loan debt, mortgage debt, health care debt: the twentieth-century promise (however hollow then) of eventual affluence in adulthood has disappeared for children before they start working.

Children today are also diagnosed as ill on a mass scale, whether in terms of the obesity "epidemic" or the "need" for children's chronic medication for anxiety, depression, and ADHD. These shifts slide onto the body and expose it to those technologies of discipline central to the formation of sexual subjectivity: namely, the cultivation of the self and the responsibility to self-govern. In short, the progressive generational ideology of the twentieth century, according to which children incarnated the future precisely because they would be healthier, richer, and happier than their parents, has now lost its purchase, however delusional it was all along. The modern fantasies of the child-figure have simply become unconvincing in the face of the material conditions of contemporary life.

This fantasy meltdown makes for strange feelings in the precincts of childhood. For children excluded from US ideals, the breakdowns of the now are not really news, much less cause for nostalgia or grief. Rather, for many children of color, queer children, trans children, immigrant children, disabled children, and poor children, the instability of futurity is finally a partial national admission that as children they *have* been excluded from these ideals. Somewhat differently, this breakdown of fantasy also cracks an opening for children outside the United States and global north. If the United States is especially guilty of exporting its idealized version of childhood as a universalizing, colonizing force, even that process is becoming stranger today than we might realize. Several of the essays collected here provincialize historical narratives of modern Anglo-American childhood. They do so by scouting situations where the state deployed a child ideal so as to induce the guaranteed failure of actual children (for instance, in Mary Zaborskis's piece, Native children in state boarding schools). Or these essays shift terrain—geographic terrain—and thus our expectations of the relation between the global south and north.

Kathryn Bond Stockton's essay, "The Queer Child Now and Its Paradoxical Global Effects," takes us deep inside these tangles. Stockton's crafted theoretical ballasts, kid Orientalism, reverse pedophilia, and manifest latency, each serve to comment, in ways that surprise, on the gaps among what adults think they know, what they want children to think and tell, and where children have moved while adults have been busy telling and thinking. Forging these new concepts, Stockton reexamines the "ghostly gay child"—a central figure from her book *The Queer Child* (2009)—to ask how it's been changing, conceptually and politically, in our current century, and whether its ghostly specificity is subsiding. How does it *now* mark every child's queerness and to what oddly global effects? Engaging these questions, Stockton speculates on something that's been surfacing in Anglo-American public culture over the last ten years or so. "A future the public fears is coming—child sexuality, evidenced by sexting, 'gay' kids in middle school, and sexual bullying—is accompanying *exportation* of a fading child (the figure of the innocent child) to other lands," where it seems available to be rediscovered. Quite paradoxically, an aesthetics of world documentaries on the-child-in-peril-in-the-third-world (a genre enjoying conspicuous success on the art-film circuit in the United States) may be "restoring" the "Western"-style innocent child through, of all things, the sexualized, racialized, "HIV child." Nonetheless, Stockton claims, this child-in-peril, this kid Orientalism, becomes a threat in a different direction. It becomes the icon of globalized poverty that makes us want to run from it, because of the demands it makes for our response. Feeling thus threatened, we flee from children whom, we imagine, are desiring us (in reverse pedophilia). Is there any antidote to these strange dynamics, especially when they center on the role of children's faces? Moreover, how does literature, especially experimental literary form in the novel *Push*, and something Stockton calls "lyrical fat" in the film *Precious*, work against this fray? Stockton finds answers among depictions of children's passion for signification—children's libidinal relationships to signifiers—and through new conceptions of (sexual) latency via the latency of signification.

Paul Amar's essay, "The Street, the Sponge, and the Ultra: Queer Logics of Children's Rebellion and Political Infantilization," leads us in equally twisting directions. Amar's expansive project lies outside the United States, in the detailed fieldwork and comparative frameworks he has developed through his work on Brazil—revisited through current events in Egypt. Amar makes the figure of the child revolutionary and the young football fanatic, "the Ultra," an animating force of his searching analysis, rather than a problem to be solved by an a priori epistemology. Amar demonstrates how the illegibility of children's actions in a revolution doubles as a blind spot in scholarly analysis. Thus, he charts how the cloak of childishness, under conditions of disenfranchisement and political infantilization, enables children's informal political, economic, and social activities. Matters of formal and informal agency thicken even further, when, as Amar shows, it falls to the pirated, circulated image of SpongeBob SquarePants to foster the dissident worlds of children after the Egyptian counterrevolution of the past several years. SpongeBob captures the anarchic energy and queer ambience of youth mobs in Egypt. Like him, children's marginality to serious matters of state in that country is revealed as dense with unanticipated significance. Child revolutionaries may be deemed marginal by the state and by the scholarly frameworks that define them, yet these margins are also incubators of twenty-first-century unruly childhood. With Amar, then, we find the movements of contemporary children within these queer and dizzying logics.

From the US child abroad to the child revolutionary working in Egypt, the issue's first half locates the child in affective relays that draw surprising connections among the security state, American popular culture, and the global south. The second half turns directly to the law and the state's overwhelming imprint on productions of sexual citizenship out of childhood. Clifford Rosky's essay, "Same-Sex Marriage Litigation and Children's Right to Be Queer," brings legal studies (by a law professor) back to *GLQ* for the first time in many years. The venue of this journal allows this legal scholar to ask what one can do as a law professor *and* a queer theorist. With the rapid jolts to the "now" of same-sex marriage litigation over the past few years in this country, Rosky's genealogy of the queer child under marriage law organizes bold discursive shifts into a captivating, telling transformation. The courts have moved from a fear of the queer child to a veritable adoption of the doctrine of "No Promo Hetero," according to which the state has no justified right in promoting heterosexuality, including in children. While mining queer theory—which has barely begun to be cited in academic legal journals—for what it might offer for tracing the limits of marriage law, Rosky shows how two recent decisions, *Perry v. Schwarzenegger* (2013) and *Obergefell v. Hodges* (2015), lay the groundwork for a law that might cultivate a child's right to be queer.

The concluding essay textures the background of children's rights or enforced fate to be deemed "queer"—via state policy. This piece considers histories in which the alchemy of race and sexuality generates a queer-child melancholy. Where Rosky illuminates the welcoming into citizenship of gay adults and children through marriage, Zaborskis, in "Sexual Orphanings," reveals Native children's enforced citizenship through the genocidal project of state boarding schools. Like Stockton's turn to *Push*, Zaborskis's turn to literature finds that the child asks us to trust in a weird slippage between the historical and the fictional. For those children whose racialized sexuality makes them historically impossible subjects, the aesthetic is just capacious enough to give them a brief form of life not entirely bound to the slow death forced on them by the settler state. Reading Tomson Highway's *Kiss of the Fur Queen* (1998) alongside the history of boarding schools in the United States and Canada, Zaborskis draws on the growing perspectives of queer Native studies. Deftly, she describes a bold double bind that eluci-dates how children can be made queer in a clearly nonempowering, devastating sense. The boarding school's predetermined heterosexualization of Native children "orphaned" them, in Zaborskis's wording, from any possible claim on an indig-enous sexuality. Just as perniciously, this institutional heterosexualization was *also* rigged to fail because it was racialized by the state and was often delivered through sexual violence, forcibly queering Native children through an estrangement con-trolled by the state. Zaborskis's rendering of sexual orphaning insists, therefore, on the difference that race makes in closing off the opportunity for indigenous sexuality to be recuperated during or after childhood. Living on through such dou-ble binds in some sense leads to *fictional* lives for the children who cannot find adequate life in the aftermath of cultural and erotic erasure.

Is it still the case, then, as Lee Edelman argued in *No Future* (2004), that it is impossible to talk about the child without discussing the politics of futurity? These four essays give us answers neither in the register of outright affirmation nor that of opposition. They respond instead by following bends in the concept of the future from within the now and from a range of disciplinary and methodological coordinates. While literary studies and queer theory are key dimensions here, we also want to underline the insights that come out of law, global studies, compara-tive political economy, and indigenous studies. "The Child Now" is motivated not only by our wish to catch up our thinking to the twenty-first century but by our kinship with a mass of work unfolding today. Without trying to classify that work and thereby restrict its scope, we instead point to links between this issue and other collections that have recently been published or are forthcoming, including *WSQ: Women's Studies Quarterly*'s recent special issue "Child," edited by Sarah Chinn and Anna Mae Duane (2015); *Monstrous Children and Childish Monsters*, edited by Markus P. J. Bohlmann and Sean Moreland (2015); and the forthcoming *Worlds of Wonder: The Queerness of Childhood*, edited by Anna Fishzon and Anas-tasia Kayiatos. We are excited to see queer studies, children's literature, and child-hood studies combine to nurture new voices from other fields in the humanities, social sciences, and elsewhere. In a different moment, these disciplines may not have seen themselves working on common problems. The overlaps and gaps that define our respective and varied work are now too obvious and too compelling to remain siloed—and far too productive to be summarized by a single issue, mono-graph, or collection.

There is less attention to psychoanalysis in this issue than has character-ized some of the landmark work that contributors nonetheless claim as impor-tant elements in the genealogy of the child now. Like the volume *Curiouser: On the Queerness of Children*, edited by Steven Bruhm and Natasha Hurley (2004), we are drawn to the many ways the child has yet to be taken up, is only beginning to be theorized, or might challenge ongoing conversations in queer studies and the liberal arts and sciences more broadly. Investigations of the posthuman might consider the strange inhumanity of human development, the way that the human, rather than a ready-made object for critique, has to be grown out of processes—pregnancy, infancy, and childhood—that are radically incommensurate with the rational subject. In many ways, these matters return to the genealogical connections between the child and the life sciences spelled out by Carolyn Steedman's pioneering work in *Strange Dislocations* (1998). Various neomaterialisms or object-oriented inquiries into the liveliness of things at nonsubjective or nonhuman scales might engage with the history of animating childish form, the ways in which plasticity or potentiality as concepts owe a debt to the biological and psychological child sciences. The child as a screen against which adults project claims about life finds literalization (as Heather Warren-Crow describes in *Girlhood and the Plastic Image* [2014]) in the bodily modulations of Lewis Carroll's Alice and her many sisters.

Our own new work carries on in this vein. In her book, *The Child to Come* (2016), Rebekah Sheldon explores how the catastrophic temporalities of climate change condense into fears over the end of human reproduction and a future without children. Such matters make strange patterns of thought against two current backdrops: the proliferation of forms-of-life in the new biology of patentable transgenics, and the new realities of increasingly constricted reproductive rights.[2] The vertiginous technologizing of these domains links to another site of public worry. Here lie generational anxieties over the idea that the digital is in some ways synonymous with youth. Here lies the fear that only children can keep pace with digital change, in ways that grant them a threatening autonomy. Turning yet elsewhere, Julian Gill-Peterson, in his book-length project on the history of transgender children, argues that the growing body of the child became the central object of the twentieth-century life sciences, particularly modern endocrinology. Gill-Peterson shows that the overwhelming plasticity of biological life, held in the sexed and gendered forms it takes, was the object of the broader eugenic project of the improvement of human stock. The radical openness of sex and gender in their embryonic and childish stages was sharply reduced to developmental trajectories. Yet this genealogy—the child in life sciences—reveals long-overlooked counterhistories of the modern body. One striking instance, he avers, involves transgender children in the 1960s and 1970s, who took up and *took on* the discourses that sought to confine them to experimental test cases for a general theory of sex and gender.

These conversations, all contemporary, *about* temporalities, touch on several profound ways in which the child—as figure, as threat, as ideal, as spoiler—changes the framing of our work in academe. The child is the hybrid creature assigned the impossible but obligatory role of crossing from nature to culture, with all the contradictions, tensions, and offshoots that ensue. In the era of biopower in which we live, the child is also the preeminent reservoir of that enigmatic signifier "life itself," the surplus forced to hold itself somewhere so as to grease the cogs of capital, biomedicine, and technoscience. Where the human is already too closed off, too settled, or too exhausted to be of use for the latter's full extractions, the child is a natural resource that promises the boundless cultivation of nature. "Gender," "sexuality," "race": the child (un)makes each of these linguistic registers by reminding us that they must be both implanted in yet grown out of the flesh of children. The uniquely intense quantum of vitality we have implanted in the child, of course, is the stuff that biopower and capital bank on. It is what promises to propel life forward into the human, if all goes well, or into the dystopian and catastrophic, if it doesn't.

A future, then. But not the one the modern child led us to expect. Instead of the futural child and its horizon, we now offer the involutions of the present, the folds in which we find ourselves. Instead of the spectacle of revelatory meaning, we offer this issue in full knowledge that the child "now" will only ghost the outlines of the child "then." And so we limn where the two now touch, and will touch again.

Notes

1. We do not mean to suggest, however, that the historical emergence of modern childhood was linear or even. For a thorough discussion of these historical and literary developments, see Sarah Chinn's *Inventing Modern Adolescence* (2008) and Marah Gubar's *Artful Dodgers* (2009). On innocence, see James Kincaid's classic *Erotic Innocence* (1998) and Kathryn Bond Stockton's elaboration on the strangeness of innocence in *The Queer Child* (2009).
2. On these two matters, see Franklin 2013 and Latimer 2013.

References

Bernstein, Robin. 2011. *Racial Innocence: Performing American Childhood from Slavery to Civil Rights*. New York: New York University Press.

Bohlmann, Markus P. J., and Sean Moreland, eds. 2015. *Monstrous Children and Childish Monsters: Essays on Cinema's Holy Terrors*. Jefferson, NC: McFarland Books.

Bruhm, Steven, and Natasha Hurley, eds. 2004. *Curiouser: On the Queerness of Children*. Minneapolis: University of Minnesota Press.

Chinn, Sarah. 2008. *Inventing Modern Adolescence: The Children of Immigrants in Turn-of-the-Century America*. New Brunswick, NJ: Rutgers University Press.

Chinn, Sarah, and Anna Mae Duane, eds. 2015. "Child." Special issue, *WSQ: Women's Studies Quarterly* 43, nos. 1–2.

Edelman, Lee. 2004. *No Future: Queer Theory and the Death Drive*. Durham, NC: Duke University Press.

Firestone, Shulamith. 1970. *The Dialectic of Sex: The Case for Feminist Revolution*. New York: William Morrow.

Fishzon, Anna, and Anastasia Kayiatos, eds. Forthcoming. *Worlds of Wonder: The Queerness of Childhood*. London: Palgrave Macmillan.

Franklin, Sarah. 2013. *Biological Relatives: IVF, Stem Cells, and the Future of Kinship*. Durham, NC: Duke University Press.

Gubar, Marah. 2009. *Artful Dodgers: Reconceiving the Golden Age of Children's Literature*. London: Oxford University Press.

Kincaid, James. 1998. *Erotic Innocence: The Culture of Child Molesting*. Durham, NC: Duke University Press.

Latimer, Heather. 2013. *Reproductive Acts: Sexual Politics in North American Fiction and Film*. Montreal: McGill-Queens University Press.

Sheldon, Rebekah. 2016. *The Child to Come: Life after the Human Catastrophe*. Minneapolis: University of Minnesota Press.

Steedman, Carolyn. 1998. *Strange Dislocations: Childhood and the Idea of Human Interiority*. Cambridge, MA: Harvard University Press.

Stockton, Kathryn Bond. 2009. *The Queer Child, or Growing Sideways in the Twentieth Century*. Durham, NC: Duke University Press.

Warren-Crow, Heather. 2014. *Girlhood and the Plastic Image*. Lebanon, NH: Dartmouth College Press.

THE QUEER CHILD NOW AND ITS PARADOXICAL GLOBAL EFFECTS

Kathryn Bond Stockton

"*G*ay" kids in middle school. Kids coming out—as what, exactly? Children sexting. Becoming sex offenders. Wanting to transition. In other countries, "swarming" or engaging revolutions. In the United States, being entrepreneurs.[1]

What I've called "the queer child" needs a new theoretical capture.[2] Now that we're squarely in the twenty-first century, we who write on childhood need new ways to approach its strangeness. To grasp "the child" where it lives liquidly, longingly, stealthily, or unconsciously in its broad array: the child queered by money, gender, sexuality, race, ghostly gayness, and imagined innocence. To grasp what continually odd dynamics surround its (charming) threats. And to grasp "it" as a fond fantasy held by adults—or a young body slipping from this fantasy, sliding to the side of it, licking it or fighting it.[3]

The theories I craft here—kid Orientalism, reverse pedophilia, manifest latency—are meant to offer a novel set of paradigms by which to make sense, *speculative* sense, of what has been happening in the United States in this new century. Indeed, I beg patience with my speculations, both their speed and breadth. They are a breathless run at effects that collide with each other; ungathered, as yet. Receive this essay as my try at gathering (humbling as it is), wedding paradoxes each to the other.[4]

What has been happening is *quite* paradoxical. And so typically Anglo-American. In fact, the "global" paradoxical effects I will describe boomerang to North American matters in their obvious blinkered partiality. (Our global, our selves.) More intriguingly, put these paradoxes next to Paul Amar's—as he discusses, later in this issue, children's rebellions, specifically in Egypt—and you will encounter a strange set of bookends. What defines them both? Something I have made axiomatic to my grasp of childhood all along: "we" fear the children we

GLQ 22:4

DOI 10.1215/10642684-3603186

© 2016 by Duke University Press

would protect. This little axiom just might connect our distinct paradoxes. What distinguishes mine from Amar's is *what* is feared, what form threat takes. Anglo-America, caught in a dream from which it won't awake, is steeped in fantasies of vaporous innocence. These are largely suburban-driven fantasies, however they seep into national discourse.[5] Thus, parental "terror" in the global north can still fixate on sexualization, worrisome signs of children's being sexual(ized): not on hordes of children taking to the streets, living in the streets, running on the loose while they protest labor conditions, dominate festivals, or rather gleefully rampage shopping malls, as they do in Egypt (Amar, this issue). Think of the "global" story I tell, then, as a ghostly ship passing in the night the ship of the boisterous children illuminated by Amar. One succinct version of my story goes like this, though it will take me this essay to unwind it, explain it, clarify it:

The United States is outsourcing its child. The "innocent child" our country is so fond of is made overseas in a very odd way, a way that turns innocence upside down, a way that even turns good old Orientalism inside out, forging a new weird version of it (kid Orientalism). We, as a public, produce this child for our own purposes, then feel justified running from it, as if its "desire" for us is threatening or somehow inappropriate (reverse pedophilia). The material needs of these children so readily feel like a kind of demanding desire to US viewers. Somewhere a child is desiring me, so I imagine, so I'm led to feel. Hence, my purple coinage—"reverse pedophilia"—stresses the feel of this threat of desire, though it is an imagined desire. It is aimed not by an adult at a child (the general public's usual worry) but by a child at an adult, though in specific ways I reveal. And thus it's actually difficult to do what I believe is ethical for sexual citizens: desire this child. Pursue this child. With all curiosity and with listening ears. Penetrate this child *in this crucial way*: get behind its face, get beyond the well-worn image of its face, push through the wall of its documented face. Why get past the face? The face, in this instance, blocks our sight, as we're going to learn. Moreover, it protects us—in ways I wish it wouldn't—from something tricky but valuable to do. This tricky thing involves our understanding, and our encountering, children's passion for signification, alongside their own sexual desires. These forms of latency—signification, sexual desire—are always present, always growing now, at this very time (manifest latency).[6]

Now step back and let's begin again. Let's explore what's happened to the function of "delay," that definitive marker of childhood for twentieth-century Anglo-Americans. The child as a creature of managed delay. Is the outsourcing of US childhood somehow driven by the waning of delay?

Whither the Child? Whither Delay?

Shrinking, receding, drying up, growing flaccid: pick your adjective. If, in Anglo-American terms, the fundamental feature of childhood is delay—delay along the path to the land of adulthood—children are not just growing astray inside delay, as once they were. Delay itself is withering. Grandly telescoping. Children are (again) growing up too soon, in someone's estimation.[7]

Now, moreover, the "ghostly gay child" may be the canary in the coal mine (yet again), set to signal this danger at hand, for those sensing danger. In *The Queer Child* (Stockton 2009), I argued children's queerness, every-child-as-queer, childhood-as-the-queerest-of-categories, based on the model of the ghostly gay child, among other versions of children's queerness.[8] This specific figure, chief among the species of children's strangeness, profoundly showed the child as a creature of delay, even as it showed a sideways growth, often a palpably sexual growth, moving inside its very suspensions. Why did I call it a creature of delay? Because it could only state itself publicly, whatever it is, as something it was—"I was a gay child"—only after its straight life died, after a teen or adult "came out." That is, the gay child was precisely ghostly because it could not live in the present tense, even though it often consciously, secretly had a relationship with the *word* gay—or with the word's vague associations and connotations, without the word itself. In this respect, the gay child dramatized, intensified the bold dynamics of delay for every child, being held up in such intense ways.

Now delay is dwindling. Increasingly, now, in Anglo-America, ghostliness is falling off the gay child. Even if children are still often secretly gay to themselves—whatever that means, whatever relating to the signifier gay does for the child or does *to* the child—parents and many in the general public are now believing that children can be gay in the present tense (whatever these folks take "being gay" to mean). Witness the *New York Times*'s feature story "Coming Out in Middle School" (2009) or the ubiquitous nature of the It Gets Better campaign for several years, with its many (albeit retrospective) tributes to gay kids.[9] As the gay child is ever more discussed, even if it's still largely birthed through retrospection, belief in its existence daily grows, as the frightened Boy Scouts ended up discovering.[10]

Then there's sexting. Child sexuality, alongside the gay child, is ever more emerging from its shadow states, to the dismay of so many parents. Stories like the one in the *New York Times*, "A Girl's Nude Photo, and Altered Lives: When Texting Turns Explicit at Fourteen, Repercussions Last" (Hoffman 2011), are offered as an exposé to anyone not in the know about such things (at that time). Indeed, a large group of US sex offenders is composed of children: kids texting pictures of their bodies to each other. More striking still, to put this matter of child-sexuality-grudgingly-recognized into context, we can consult *Newsweek*'s "Sex and the Single Tween"—a 2014 cover story. As a subheading trumpets: "'*They grow up so fast' used to be a wistful sigh; now it's a panicked cry for help from parents watching their 10-year-old daughters critique Miley Cyrus's twerking and discuss oral sex with their friends*" (Jones 2014: 1). Perhaps to achieve maximum fright, or just to highlight kids that matter to *Newsweek*'s grip on cultural change, the journalist interviews parents and girls in suburban Boston.[11]

As the piece opens, the tweens "are discussing boys, Lady Gaga and blow jobs," and also who, at age eleven, is dating whom and "what sexy means" (Jones 2014: 1). Writes the journalist, "No matter what the topic, their conversation always seemed to come back to sex": "'Do men measure their penises?' 'Do girls care how big they are?' 'Are you getting married?' 'Are you a virgin?'" (ibid.: 2). Laments one parent, "What my 8-year-old [daughter] is interested in is exactly what my 14-year-old [daughter] is interested in. . . . she wants the bras, she wants the thongs" (ibid.: 15). To get at "the hyper-sexualization of young girls," the article catalogs the media and messages "aimed" at these children: for example, "the 2008 poster advertisements for the TV show *Gossip Girl* had taglines like 'Every Parent's Nightmare' and 'Mind-Blowingly Inappropriate' alongside images of characters in passionate embraces" (ibid.: 3). Making these tweens potentially more dangerous are their own media habits and spending: "Eight-to-10-year-olds average five and a half hours of media use a day"—often from their pockets—and "America's twenty million tweens wield $43 billion in annual spending" (ibid.: 10, 13). The upshot? Says an expert the article cites: "Latency—the developmental period when adult yearnings and sexual urges are dormant, waiting to be awakened in adolescence—has evaporated" (ibid.: 24). The author herself states: "The result terrifies many adults: American women, age tween" (ibid.: 4). Overall, the sentiment of interviewed parents appears to be this: where did that precious delay go? Sex is finding kids, targeting them, but they don't seem to desire our protections. The author summarizes this perceived predicament, essaying that "tweens today are constantly exposed to the seemingly impossible expectation of being innocent and sexual simultaneously" (ibid.: 9). One can almost hear a collective plea from parents, at least these parents, who are crying out: is there a child somewhere who is innocent and, yes, maybe sexual, and *wants* our protections?

Enter "third world" children in peril. There's a whole genre of world documentary devoted to them, since about 2000.[12] And maybe they're having paradoxical effects, which are being driven by the queer children (the range of queer children) I've been discussing. Maybe children-quite-experienced-in-peril are, without their knowing it, restoring our public's stubborn longing for innocent children who need our protections and want our protections. That's one paradox I present: experienced children become the face of innocent children, in this genre. The second paradox will not surprise anyone: many Americans want this idea of the child in peril without the demands of the actual child. God forbid these children pursue us, importune us, or tell us something sexual we don't want to hear. Sadly, then, as I explain, these art-house documentaries don't make it easy to reach these children, receive these children, outside this dynamic and its set of paradoxes. For all their formal experimentation, these documentaries mostly guarantee that their viewers will get blocked at the level of the face—by children's faces—and at the level of visual images in general, as I demonstrate.

Is there any hope, then, to reach around these barriers? Somehow to encounter a *manifest* latency that can take account of child sexuality? That can respect the foundational dictum concerning signification in itself: "the latency with which everything signifiable is struck as soon as it is raised . . . to the function of a signifier?" (Lacan 1982: 82).[13] Indeed, one recalls that both Jacques Lacan and Jacques Derrida embraced Ferdinand de Saussure's idea of the signifier because it evinces the structure of desire. The all-important, unclosable gap between the signifier and the meanings-on-delay that attach to it gives meaning-making the structure of longing and—so fitting for "children," as I show—the structure of latency. Might we desire to listen to this latency? In this essay, I confront something not getting named as I would name it: children's relationship to the signifier. I want to deem this attachment libidinal, sensuous, even sexual.[14] Thus I wish to visit a novel, *Push* (Sapphire 1997), and its appearance as the film *Precious* (2009), as a counterforce in Anglo-America, a powerful corrective to world documentaries on children in crisis. These documentaries' (varying) inabilities to render or imagine children's intimate relationships to signifiers of their own choosing tell a new postcolonial tale that *Push* and *Precious* urgently and passionately, if unintentionally, push back against.

Push is more powerful than *Precious* on these fronts. As the written text, *Push* performs remarkable, fascinating feats of voicing latency and children's passion for signification. Oddly, what I deem the impossible narration of the novel *Push* is the very key to its conveying latency. *Precious*, the film, will pulse at strategic moments in this argument but achieves its focus only at the end, in my essay's coda. There, its unique visual qualities are considered. And there also, I explain why the film works for me, against all odds. To put it in a nutshell that needs explaining: what specifically blocks our view of children in the documentary films is the face—something *Precious* undermines with fascinating fat, lyrical fat. To the extent that Precious's fat steals the focus from her face—insofar as fat is *heard*—*Precious* makes its mark. Even so, a paradox of representing agency awaits us at the close.[15]

Children's Passion Coming, Coming Out On Paper

"that the voice, that writing, be as fresh . . . lubricated, delicately
granular and vibrant as an animal's muzzle"
—Roland Barthes, *The Pleasure of the Text*

> **everi mornin**
> by Precious j.
>
> Everi mornin
> i write
> a poem
> before I go to
> school
> marY Had a little lamb
> but I got a kid
> an HIV that folow me
> to school
> one day.
> —from the novel *Push*, by the poet Sapphire

What might come with a sexual child? Something that doesn't look sexy at all: a passion for the signifier, which Lacan and Derrida have said is doomed to latency: something that marks where longing and longings-to-mean reside, where they lurk and linger, fattening if also hiding on a page.

Lyrical lurking, lyrical lingering, and lyrical fat. Even a leaning-sideways into a longing for language (with all its latency) and the right to literacy. Picture for a moment a large black girl, pregnant by her father for now the second time, infected by him with HIV, abused by her mother, and functionally illiterate. That is, picture Precious. Onscreen these matters are carried by—bam!—an image sequence out of nowhere, hitting film viewers upside their heads: the mother throws an object at her daughter's skull; cut to sweaty father loosening his belt; Precious on bed now; view of bedsprings creaking, rocking; eggs are sizzling in grease in a pan; Vaseline; rape; Precious launching fantasies of being a movie star flouncing, sashaying down a red carpet. . . . You can surely see how viewers might despise the terms of this film as melodramatic, over the top, possibly campy, sensational renderings of sexual harm. I see why. I see their power and potential to repel, especially intellectually. But I'd like the film to pivot on the novel, suggesting currents counter to repulsion.[16]

Strikingly, in fact, for all this sexual, sexualized sensation, novel and film smartly conceptualize how this abuse interferes with *literacy*. How this sexual abuse is matched by state neglect of children's education, making the state a sexual abuser of a girl's longing for signification. And, as I show, how a girl's longing, her sexual agency, comes out on paper as a form of latency.[17] "Latent": "present or potential, but not manifest," says the *American Heritage Dictionary*, as in *latent talent*, *latent sexuality*, *latent meaning*, or *latent period* ("the incubation period of [a] . . . disease"). Synonyms: "dormant" and "quiescent." From a Precious poem: "amung the vakent trees / is secirt plots / of green diamonds / call grass" (Sapphire 1997: 145). Precious sees dormancy and speaks to it poetically, making scenes of vacancy secretly jeweled with growth and fertility. And in the novel this passion is pushed. With death lurking, while she's getting bigger, deep in her pregnancy and HIV, Precious longs for poetry. She would write poems.

Fascinating quandaries assail us from the start. What does it mean that a poet/author (namely, Sapphire) writes in the novel fictional poems for a poet/character (namely, Precious), a character who narrates throughout the whole novel how she is emerging into literacy, via her passion and struggle for language? Just to state the obvious: an adult author is throwing her own voice into and as the passionate voice of a sexual child, a poetic teen/child who is writing poems.[18] But the novel's setup proves more conceptual the more one takes it at face value. Sapphire's Precious character is the imagined *voice* of a latency. It is a truly impossible voice as it sits on the page at the novel's start, even inside the novel's own terms, since it is a written voice that tells how it's emerging into written signs, as if latency could speak and write itself. So when I write "Precious" throughout this essay, you will see me naming an impossibility from its very face.[19]

Moreover, I am naming something more alluring than the fiction of a girl/child "expressing herself" in poetry and prose, though the novel sounds like expression to readers. Precious, rather, is a book-length tonal stack, a collection of tones that *expresses latency*—so fitting for the *concept*, the concept of the mystery, of a sexual child, as I show.[20] In the speakings that are Precious, sounding like a teen/child, we find dramatized the sexual and economic politics—and passion—of children's latent relationships with signifiers, with writing most of all, which allows for words to hover round a page, and for their meanings to fatten as they hover in their suspension. Something else emerges in poems, as we know: the sonic pulse of signifiers: their alluring sound and tickings of time, granular and vibrant. Or as Precious puts it: "go into the poem / the HEART of it / beating / like / a clock / a virus / tick / tock" (177).

Viral Clock

Slide with me now to a certain kind of child that Precious represents: "the HIV child": the child with a signifier, HIV, signifying sex (or drugs or blood) and often race: a sexual(ized) child in a racialized world: a child with a bomb that may go off inside.[21]

    Given this potential ticking away, this kind of child dramatizes latency in a threatening way, since "latency" or "interval" in 1987, when *Push* is set, formed a distinguishing medical feature of the designation HIV-positive. HIV was not only the infection of a body with the virus that causes AIDS (as it still is). It was also medically conceived as the interval between infection and manifest symptoms (as it may be). For this reason, HIV, in the absence of symptoms, was and can be a strange state of latency, a manifest latency, in which you are ill with an idea, the lurking idea of your possible death. (In 1987, death seemed a certainty.) This kind of latency makes you enter a strange temporality: it may make you nostalgic for yourself even before you begin to decline. You find you fall ill with *nostalgia* for a *future*, a time in which you clearly saw a future before you, before you felt the "tick tock" of a viral clock. And yet, now there's "dormancy" as the path that HIV might also take, since "HIV can lie dormant indefinitely," according to the researcher William Haseltine (quoted in Kaiser 1993: 3), hidden from a person's own immune system, but still lurking inside their cells.[22]

    How does the HIV child or teen intensify this drama? By *growing* with the virus. In 1996, when *Push* was published, almost half of children with HIV in the United States were "growing up" with AIDS and HIV, living with their viral infection, which was making them strangely . . . threatening.[23] Here's what we read in the *New York Times*, as early as 1993, in a piece titled "Growing Up in the Shadow of the AIDS Virus" (Navarro 1993): "In a medical building in the Bronx, two girls and a boy sit around a table . . . chattering—about summer camp, Michael Jackson and, in between, the virus that has haunted each of them since birth. Once . . . growing up with H.I.V. meant mostly repeated trips to doctors. . . . But the boy . . . is now

13, and the girls . . . are 11—old enough that the virus has now become a cause for fears about infecting others, about having a future, about premature death."

First in this list is sexual threat. The HIV child may threaten others. And, by the way, reports mostly focus on the black child, who in the United States since the early nineties has been the face of the HIV child. (Ryan White, a white child who contracted HIV in 1984 through a blood transfusion, was the face of the virus early on, in the United States, before he died in 1990.)[24] In another piece from the *New York Times*, from 1999, three years after the appearance of *Push*, we meet a black boy and his siblings, who are "part of a maturing, little-understood population of infected children who, because of medical advances, are living far longer than anyone expected" (Richardson 1999: 1). "Now, instead of planning funerals," says the *Times*, "parents . . . worry that their children's behavior could hurt them, and—if unprotected sex is involved—others" (ibid.). "Parents . . . face a whole new set of problems. . . . 'They thought the child was going to die' [explains a medical director in the Bronx]. 'There's an ambivalence that the kids are doing well. They have invested so much to try to keep the kids healthy and now the kids are taking their fate into their own hands. They're making risky choices'" (2). Indeed, in a much more recent case, in 2011, a case now settled and decision reversed, a "child" with HIV—once again, a black youth, age thirteen—was not admitted to the Milton Hershey School in Pennsylvania, since, said the school, this boy "pose[d] a direct threat to the health and safety of others" (Stamm 2011: 2). Why? "We are serving children, and no child can be assumed to always make responsible decisions which protect the well-being of others" (3). More specifically, wrote a reporter, a school spokeswoman "said the school was most worried the boy would have sex" (Newcombe, Claiborne, and Ramsey 2011: 3).

"Ambivalence that the kids are doing well." Here, evidently, was and still is a latency scarier than HIV: the manifest latency, the not-so-latent latency, of child sexuality that US culture is being forced to reckon with ever more steadily in this new century. And yet, for a century, Anglo-American cultures have deemed the child to *be* a latency, a certain kind of interval, as I have stated, that the general public thinks it can "protect." The public has been busy protecting an interval (as much as anything) by delaying children's access to sex, labor, and adult linguistic codes, as I have explained in *The Queer Child*. I am speaking, of course, of the child made strange though appealing to us by its all-important innocence. Here is why "innocent" children are strange. They are protected from what they *approach*: the adulthood against which they must be defined. Adults walk the line—the impossible line—of keeping the child at once what it is (what adults are not) and leading it toward what it cannot (at least, as itself) ever be (what adults are). Innocent children are seen as normative but also not like us, at the same time. And this normative strangeness may explain why children, simply as an idea, are likely to be white and middle class. It is a privilege to need to be protected and thus to have a childhood. Because of privilege, then, the all-important feature of weakness sticks to these signs (white and middle class) and helps signal innocence.[25]

Here are two problems. By making children innocent, we've made children foreign, obscure to us. So, in some respects, the innocent child is the queerest child of all, the one least like the adults who retrospect it. Nonetheless, this foreignness finds itself beloved in the United States. Here is a foreignness actually embraced. Thus more troubling to normative views have been notions like "the gay child" or "the child of color" (who may be the same child)—and the HIV child. These are children who for many years, before the more recent worries over sexual tweendom, have been spotlighting every child's darkness, every child's queerness, through their propensity for growing astray inside the delay that defines who they are. Dangerous in their movements *from within their latency*, these kinds of children outline the pain, closets, emotional labor, sexual motives, and sideways movements that attend all children, albeit in highly various ways.

How, then, do we (the general public seems to be saying) protect ourselves from our realizations, our growing hesitations, surrounding children's sideways growth, surrounding the dangers they present to us? By doing something odd. We seek their endangerment ever more fervently—as something we can protect them against. Pedophile hysteria has been quite good for this. But so has the somewhat recent documentary urge to film the child-in-peril in various places around the globe. And this endeavor, as I show, returns us to the child's relationship to signifiers, which returns us to Precious and her poetry—Precious as an antidote to a certain strain of world documentaries.[26]

Kid Orientalism and the Signs of Reverse Pedophilia

This could sound outlandish. I confess ignorance as I stake my claims. I don't know the motives that drive these documentaries in their creation and their production and their range of sophisticated renderings. Rather, I'm stressing effects they make available and how these affect the liquid idea of the sexual child.[27] I am suggesting that documentaries on the child-in-crisis in India, Malawi, and Uganda—depicting children imperiled by sex trade, civil war, and AIDS—are for many viewers relocating the "Western"-style innocent child to foreign soil, where it can strangely be rediscovered.[28] That is, it can appear that these urgent films, through a loving backslap, grant their child protagonists the privilege of weakness that only these children's extraordinary peril can produce. So, paradoxically, we may look for "our" child, "our" disappearing child—the child who needs protection, the child who wants protection—where we should know, where we do know, the Western-child-on-its-long-delay cannot be found. More paradoxically, because of these films' obvious anti-Orientalist impulses, they are forging a new Orientalism. Kid Orientalism, which runs along the track of a new kind of logic but reproduces US obsessions. How can this be?

Recall that Orientalism, as Edward Said (1979) defined it over three decades ago (using the terms *East* and *West*), involves the West's construction, to its own advantage, of the Orient as a negative inversion of the West, creating an ontological distinction between the Orient and the Occident, such that all Eastern societies are seen as fundamentally similar to each other and dissimilar to the West. Moreover, orientalism, as you'll recall, is fashioned by means of literature and/or historiographies that misunderstand, or misrepresent, life in the East. Are these films, then, the Oscar-winning *Born into Brothels* (2004), the Academy-nominated, beautiful *War Dance* (2007), and Madonna's art-house documentary, *I Am Because We Are* (2008), focusing on children orphaned by AIDS, infected by AIDS, in the African country Malawi, Orientalist by Said's definition? No, not really. None of these films feature the negative inversion of the West. Nor do they use literary texts and historical records that falsify the postcolonial histories of these countries. Moreover, these films do not craft divides, ontological or epistemological, between their settings and Western sensibilities. Quite the opposite in one respect. Madonna in her film grandly connects all human concern, human experience, through the suffering figure of the child—here the unifying figure of the child, whom, she presumes, we immediately recognize.

But this is not "our" innocent child. Nor is this our troubling child, who is taking her fate into her hands. This is a version of our troubling child with its bold suffering returned upon its head, where its harm can act like a wash, soaping, rinsing, buffing suffering into a sheen we can read as weakness and thus as innocence. This is how we get this Platonic Child, a child preserved in amber, fossilized or etherized, but breathing and living in Malawi all along, we're led to believe; someone requiring no translation or explanation because we've known this child in Washington or Paris. (Never mind that we are bemoaning that "our" children—the presumptive models for Malawi's children-just-like-ours—have fled the scene of US childhood, spurning the need for public protection.) Still, Madonna asks, "Aren't these the fears and hopes of any child?" after her film has shown us a context that bears scant resemblance to anything we've known, if we're not Mala-

wians or those who know Malawi, where, the film instructs us, one million children
orphaned by AIDS (out of the country's twelve million people) seem to be everywhere: "living on the streets, sleeping under bridges, hiding in . . . buildings, being
abducted, kidnapped, raped," circumstances leading to "a state of emergency."
This is the crux of kid Orientalism, which is largely anti-Orientalism with a significant and perverse twist. Anti-Orientalism, in this case, comes through children's
unquestioned universalism that denies the differences the films themselves imply
(historical, cultural, conceptual differences in the lives of children lived in these
countries), the differences that make them of cinematic interest. Most perversely, it
is these very differences in the lives of children—their unique forms and degrees
of suffering, according to these films—that may make them, in the eyes of viewers, supercandidates for Western-style innocent children who, above all, need our
protection. A flattened version of US childhood—one we have had to start doubt-
ing ourselves—is thus magically restored on foreign soil, through (of all things) the
sexualized, racialized, HIV child.[29]

Is this Orientalism? The theory of orientalism perhaps collapses under the
weight of its own contradictions, as seen here where anti-Orientalism spawns Orientalism. Yet my failed formula—kid Orientalism—reveals the new pressure to
universalize the child precisely by outsourcing childhood innocence to those countries (once) Orientalized: countries considered "undeveloped" (childish? just developing?) that once were thought to be without children worthy of being like Western
children. However, unlike the "noble savage" dynamics of old—the Orientalism
that discovers lost Edens in the East, among native people treated like children
by their colonizers—these new innocents are innocent through peril. They are
technically inverted-innocents-in-their-experience, to put the matter oddly, if one
would use these terms. It thus takes tremendous disavowal to find "our" child, as
I have suggested. Perhaps one could say that kid Orientalism is the full flowering
of the contradictions long lying latent in the West's treatment of the "developing"
countries of the world, bound to come to a head in a crisis over "children."

Is this Orientalism? It doesn't really matter. It's a dilemma for signification.
In the end, Madonna's film cannot produce a signifier I haven't seen all of my life,
though I have never seen these children. I mean that image glazing our eyes, the
one many viewers will know from CARE or UNICEF ads since *their* childhood (me
on Halloween with my UNICEF box, collecting coins for this image in my head).
You know the image. A glossy reproduction of a glassy stare, in high definition;
lassitude with "resilience" (Madonna's favorite word), resilience hard to see even if
I know it's there. Completely strange to say, each child's face—its most personal,
most tender signifier—makes me not see the child I am viewing. I can't see these

children because these children are blocking my view—of them, themselves. This grim tautology meets and defeats my gaze at every turn, making me try, as Madonna's viewer, to do an impossible visual maneuver: stiff-arm the signifier, stiff-arm the child, so as to slip behind its face, to see *around* what the signifier's showing me. And not telling me. Stashed behind each image, so it feels to me, is a "vakent, secrit plot," as Precious might put it: a growing dormancy.

What does it mean in this country for so many children to wear, in their illness or their orphanhood, a sexual and sexually stigmatizing signifier HIV/AIDS, which is highly stigmatizing in *their* country? How do they think about it? What would they say about it? At one fascinating point in the film, we hear the startling story of a young teen girl whose child has died of AIDS and who herself must now be "cleansed," according to her tribe, by having sex with a married shaman three times a day, until he says she's cured. The teen/child asks: "Will I continue to live like this forever?" There's a world of signification lurking here, but this is all we get. In *Born into Brothels*, there likewise seems a remarkable story yet to be told by the children themselves. What do they grasp about their mothers' work, which is largely performed inside the home, just beyond a curtain's veil dropped inside a room? What do they think about the futures planned for them, which for the girls involve this work? What does it mean for their or their brothers' sexual imaginations as children?

Patterns emerge as one becomes immersed in the genre of these films. First, to the extent these documentaries cannot forge new relationships for the film's viewer or for these children with their world of signifiers, these documentaries give us kid Orientalism (notwithstanding my problems with this phrase I myself have coined). Second, one sees why documentaries of children capture less of children than do fictions of fictionalized children. Finally, we understand why these films all give us uplift narratives to soothe our encounter with these children's pain. It's not just the wish to make children something other than victims, which of course is laudable. It's a concession to Western heartbreak—the filmmakers' fear of breaking *our* hearts—which we might feel threatened with and so might cause our turning away (the filmmakers' nightmare).

Eminently possible in this circumstance is what I am calling reverse pedophilia. (Somewhere a child is desiring me. . . . I believe, I feel . . .) This strange dynamic is a bold enactment of Lacan's assertion that organic need becomes encased inside demand, disappears into the soup of demand, as need is vectored by language to an Other. This encasing, this vectoring, leads to desire, which is the gap between need and demand, leading to dynamics that for the film's viewer might go like this: where I see need, I feel demand, as a kind of language, a kind of desire, directed at me that I can't answer.[30] In an article I've written, I explore a novel, *The Hour of the Star* (1977), by Latin America's premier woman novelist, Clarice Lispector, who adopts the voice of a male narrator who's writing a novel about a real girl from the poverty-stricken, racialized backwoods of Brazil, whom he's glimpsed only once. ("Why should I write about a young girl whose poverty is so evident?" "She has clung to my skin like viscous glue. . . . [She] doesn't want to get off my back" [Lispector 1992: 21].) His narration cuts to the heart of the need-always-already-aimed-at-me-as-demand-in-my-mind that I'm suggesting haunts these films. Here's how he voices it: "The girl worries me so much that I feel drained. She has drained me empty. And the less she demands, the more she worries me. I feel frustrated and annoyed. A raging desire to smash dishes and break windows. How can I avenge myself? Or rather, how can I get satisfaction? I've found the answer: by loving my dog who consumes more food than she does" (25–26). Here is this logic in a nutshell, then, the logic these films must struggle against: I see need / I see a will to live / I feel it as demand that I cannot satisfy / I get angry / I turn to my dog.

How Can These Kids Compete with Dogs?
What Reverses Reverse Pedophilia?

No wonder these films each have their own way of keeping up our spirits with their kids' resilience, long enough to move us toward these children's "innocence" shown by the extremity of their experience. *Born into Brothels* takes a clever tack. The children whom we follow are each given cameras and taught still photography by the movie's filmmakers, in the clear hope of showing these children's latent talents and showing them showing us how they see the world. But the film begins with its own camera work, giving us close-ups of the children's faces—close-cropped, shadowed, turned to the light—that resonate strongly with African images and, I would say, impede our gaze. Then the movie-camera snakes with an undulating, sinister motion through the darkened alleys where the brothels hide, while a voice tells us "it's almost impossible to photograph in the red-light district." This confession makes us hope that what the children photograph will be especially telling, will take us beyond the intriguing hints of their thoughts embedded in fragments that we hear: "one has to accept life as being sad and painful—that's all"; "I need to make a living and take care of my sister"; "my father tried to sell me"; "I know what [my mother] does for work . . . and I feel bad talking about these things"; "[my friend has] talked to me about it many times . . . and asked me not to tell anyone."

These oral fragments (seductive, incomplete) remain the film's most illuminating signifiers, because the kids' cameras do not show us anything the filmmakers' cameras aren't showing, too. Here we hit the glass of tautology again, crashingly stopped by *visual signifiers blocking our sight*, a blockage now produced from a different angle. Think of a box inside a box inside a box. In fact, quite literally, the film's movie-camera films a kid-with-camera taking a picture; the film then develops before our eyes, as if the children's pictures are sophisticated Polaroids that nakedly, suddenly reveal themselves to sight, but only as the movie's camera lets them. More inside the box: the photographs the filmmakers film as selections of the kids' work, as indications of their latent talent—often striking stills in burnished black and white or saturated color of some street scene—become indistinguishable from the aestheticized, art-house photographs viewers have seen of these locales, and which the kids are sweetly, generously led, without bad faith, to reinvent (for a show titled "Through the Eyes of a Child"). "Seeing through their eyes," therefore, leads us tautologically not only to what we have just been seeing from the movie-camera but also to what we could see at Sotheby's, where their photographs are later sold. The film's trailer itself says as much: "led by the compassion of one woman . . . from the streets of Calcutta to an auction block at Sotheby's . . . the story of a [woman's] courageous vision and the children who made it happen." Perhaps no surprise: the children's latent talent enacts the *film's* vision, in a subtle inversion of purpose.

Indeed, we realize that what the film captures more than anything else, what the kids capture, with talent, with their cameras, is the steady stream of signifiers aimed at them, entering them, coming through the viewfinder, penetrating children's eyes in this context, in a kind of child-invagination of sexual signification, taking place through their eyeballs or their earholes. If only we could *hear* about what they see. We never get to hear, never get behind the face. Therefore, if the children's wielding of their cameras shows us anything, it shows us something (no small thing) that photography theory doesn't theorize: children's pleasure in the act of taking pictures with an instrument privileged adults treat as powerful and producing signifiers they or others value, even if pain rides the wave of the image. For as much as anything, these kids are drawn to what comes with these cameras: trips to the zoo; to the beach; playtime; gallery exhibitions. And they blushingly learn to see that what you frame you somehow own, as they are possessed by the cameras framing them.

War Dance almost seems hip to these problems. Hip to the problem of the overused face and hip to the need to loosen children's tongues. Since the film's topic is war, not sex, this loosening is possible. In the face of violence, we let children speak. Moreover, this film ups the ante on uplift, as it shows northern

Ugandan children preparing to perform for a music festival in their nation's capital. These are children who have lost their parents to murders by rebels or themselves have murdered at the rebels' orders to kill or be killed. Strikingly, as I've implied, the filmmakers almost seem to thematize the matter of the well-worn face by dramatizing it. In fact, each child stands firmly planted in front of the camera, slightly off-center, with an unnerving matter-of-factness, or just a you-don't-know-me stance—a posture of let-me-stiff-arm-you-before-you-find-yourself-blocked-by-my-face, a posture of don't-even-think-I-want-you, a posture almost able to reverse the dynamics of reverse pedophilia, as she or he narrates atrocities.

As the stories hit us, unfold around our ears, the camera often takes us gently into the Ugandan bush. In its move from face to foliage, the visual register is throwing in the towel (in a helpful way), confessing there's no image to match the children's words. Nothing looks sinister—just intense and, at times, intensely beautiful, even when the weather's storming, slamming, or the movie-camera gives us a spider eating flies in silhouette. Yellow-green grass is often framed against blue-black sky of remarkable density; a mottled moon shows up against cerulean. Most of the colors are bright, not hot; only intermittently does anything look heated at the sky's rim. But the saturation of these colors is arresting, especially at metallic twilight. And we have the children speaking to us, sometimes at the camera, sometimes as a disembodied voice speaking over the image of them with them looking smack at us or standing with their backs to us: "the deaths I saw were terrifying"; "I haven't had the courage yet to tell anyone what really happened out there." One girl tells of being taken by a rebel to a place by a tree where a pot was cooking something: "When I saw my mother's head being pulled from the pot," the girl calmly states, "I felt like I was losing my mind"; "there's now nothing more I can say." Later, a xylophone-playing boy with Donald Duck emblazoned on his shirt stands before us and narrates his abduction in chilling detail (with these same signifiers—bush, trees, navy-blue sky—and one abandoned building, along with a hoe, to adorn his words): "The rebels ordered us to kill [some] farmers with their own hoe; anyone caught covering their face would be killed [along] with the farmers; we started beating the backs of their heads over and over; their legs were kicking but their heads were not moving. . . . You are the first to know I have killed."

Several things are striking here. The African-child stock image I'm familiar with is finally on the move in some new way. The same signifiers used for children seeing murder are used for children made to murder, coloring innocence (if we're clinging to it) with new shades of tortured self-knowledge, even self-fragmentation and lifelong memories of bodily actions that will lurk inside one's skin, whatever one does with them. If the topic here were sexuality—rape, let's say (children raped or made to rape)—I doubt we'd get the chance to encounter, even slantwise, *nonpictorially*, these textured narratives of violence from the children. (This film is PG; *Born into Brothels* is rated R because some mothers use sexually laced profanity.) Finally, for all of this film's bold use of trauma signifiers that confess their lack of visual signifying, even though they're visual (grass and sky), the film *can* hint at the children's latent talent. It does so by rendering their bodily production—determined, consenting, disciplined, ecstatic—of sonic signifiers, rhythmic and visual, as they dance and sing at length onscreen (and against the backdrop of many other tribal-specific performances). True, their signifiers are held inside established genres of dance, instrumentals, even song, and the resilience story of their music is certainly aimed at audience uplift, but something is pointing to another level here. We are sensing that many kinds of signifiers incubate and hide inside a child, as they become a passionate part of children's intimate, even sensuous, bodily emissions. Speaking of which . . .

Sensuous Signifiers and Aggressive Faces: Fiction's "HIV Child"

It is time to circumvent the face that blocks our sight and simplifies our grasp of the children before us. It is time to have a face—even the idea of children's faces—aggress against us without our imagining reverse pedophilia. And it is time for the least tame scenes of children's incubations and their embodiment of manifest latency, a latency tied to sex and signs.

On this front, you would be forgiven if you had always thought that AIDS poetics surrounding children would be maudlin and scarcely queer. Yet two lyrical novels may persuade us to think again. Moreover, by the *ways* they take on race, they help conceptualize the issues of latency, sideways growth, and moving suspensions that at times accompany HIV status and battles with AIDS. Lending more surprise, we will find what is gleaned from reading HIV into texts where it's not (Toni Morrison's *Beloved*) and reading through and past HIV where it is (Sapphire's *Push*).

But first a word on poems, which are dramatized bundles of manifest latency. It seems de rigueur to say in introductions that modernist poets, writing in reaction to ornate diction, sought to bring poetry "to the layman" and favored forms such as brief, compressed lyrics. Moreover, their technical innovation was their sound—achieved in free verse—matched by their complicated view of the self: the dislocation of a person from voice and expression *through* sound. A making of meaning from dislocation and fragmentation. And manifest latency: the making manifest of meaning-as-latent in simple surface. Paradoxically, complexity was achieved by brevity, simplicity, succinctness. Hence, Ezra Pound's *ABC of Reading* (1934) and F. S. Flint's (1913) insistence on direct treatment of the thing, common-speech language, and complete freedom of subject matter. And hence the claim of William Carlos Williams (quoted in Kenner 1983: 2) that he made his poems from the "speech of Polish mothers." The hyperliteral and the spare could point to found-poetry found anywhere—poems hiding in plain sight on the unencumbered surface of language. Or as Precious writes in one of her poems:

> downtwn
> sky opn
> blu legs
> for
> sun.
> (Sapphire 1997: 104)

What kind of modernist poetry is this? Can a pregnant teen, a child who is with child, who is HIV positive, stand as the sign of the latency of poetry, poetry lurking around inchoate language, lurking inside the beats of time, and lurking in meanings that grow fat? Somehow poetry, HIV, and childhood share key concepts at their core. One specific linkage is latency, of course. And, as I've implied, metaphorically and literally children can stand for the vagaries of latency: what lies lurking in the body, in history, in words, in the mind. *Beloved* and *Push* each leverage latency.

In "Prophylactics and Brains: Slavery in the Cybernetic Age of AIDS," I have rather fancifully suggested reading *Beloved* as an AIDS book, a novel set back in the 1870s, just after slavery, but birthed by Morrison in 1987, the year the AIDS quilt also appeared.[31] This is a novel all about latency: the agency of latency: the viral spreading of slavery's latent, haunting remains, the kind that down the line affects girls like Precious—and any of us. Beloved herself, the novel's precious child, signifies this spread. She is a signifier standing for slavery's faceless dead and missing persons—"60 million or more," states the novel (Morrison 1987: author's dedication). As a tender signifier, but a no less aggressive signifier, Beloved is the face of slavery's threatening latency because she is the *concept* of slavery's threatening latency, suggesting that it is perversely intimate, familial, and confusedly bound to things beloved. Profoundly, it is bound to parent-child relations, which both novelists, Sapphire and Morrison, refuse to sentimentalize however they poeticize.

Let me put it this way: untimely death and the latency of deathliness—as have attached and still can attach to HIV and the HIV child—adhere to this strange baby-teen named Beloved. She is the face of untimely death. She is a baby murdered by her mother, in order to be saved from a future of enslavement. And she first appears as the ghost of a baby haunting her mother. Then, in a more unusual form—really, in an impossible form—thus in a more conceptual form, Beloved returns as a teenage baby, at the age she would have been had she lived, to invade, *in a fluids exchange*, her mother's present life, opening her mother to viral memories. (It is a stunning scene, to put it mildly. When Beloved's mother sees Beloved's face, she uncontrollably has to urinate. Running to the outhouse, she doesn't make it, voiding her urine in plain view. At the same time, Beloved is in the house, drinking cup after cup of water, since she is now infected with cholera.) Indeed, Beloved infects her mother with memories of Beloved's future, making her mother ill with nostalgia for a future, for a time her mother thought her daughter had a future, sending this mother sadly into symptoms: fevers, lassitude, dementia, a general wasting away, all on the AIDS list. And these symptoms pool while Beloved, pregnant as a baby-teen from her mother's boyfriend, becomes a dormant, threatening force by the novel's end. She's run out of town but said to be endlessly roaming the woods—the sign of slavery's viral dormancy, its manifest latency.

Here, in *Beloved*, we are not given the well-worn face of kid Orientalism, which we need for innocence *and* then need, pathetically, to sidestep by quite pitifully defending ourselves against reverse pedophilia: our imagination of a child's desire for us. *Beloved*'s dynamics are way too aggressive. They won't soothe. Rather, they imagine gothic versions of the general public's self-soothing measures. In fact, my reading of *Beloved* has been my wish to understand Morrison's making the mother, Sethe, have an autoimmune reaction to her daughter's face, a dead daughter's face, as if her memories make her ill with interval. Then there's Beloved's poetic narration (all of five pages) of her threatening seeking of her mother, as if Morrison only momentarily has given voice to latency—latent, viral memory—making it speak as a halting, not-quite-literate child: "All of it is now it is always now there will never be a time when I am not crouching and watching others who are crouching too the man on my face is dead . . . his eyes are locked . . . I see me swim away" (Morrison 1987: 210). Here we encounter Beloved in her memory of the middle passage (she speaks of coming out of blue water): Beloved awash on the sea of the dead in a time that threatens to be only now. More to the point, Beloved, it seems, has returned to her mother in search of her face, Beloved's face in her mother's mind, where, as a memory, Beloved can be thought, be demanded as a thought, and be a signifier in her mother's brain: "I have to have my face . . . my face is coming . . . she knows I want to join she chews and swallows me" (213).

What does *Push* demand? Not a battle at the face. Its contestations surround incubations. Pregnancy, virus, the latency of signification itself. And, like Beloved, Precious on the page takes unusual form—impossible form, conceptual form—as the voice of Latency. As a halting, illiterate child.

Now I want to limn the poetics of *Push*—briefly, suggestively, only provisionally. I want to limn *Push* against this backdrop of *Beloved* and the documentaries that erase or undermine the manifest latency of child sexuality—what is on the move inside this threatening latency—that *Push* shows, truly unveils.[32] Penned by a poet, the novel *Push*, which became *Precious* when it hit the screen, gives us, like *Beloved*, but throughout the book, a narrating, pregnant, poetic teen/child (also like Beloved pregnant by her mother's lover, who in this case is her own father). This child personifies HIV in 1987 when the novel's set and, like Beloved, is locked in titanic struggle with her mother. Here, however, Precious's mother *resembles* the state, actively causing her daughter's harm, owning, as it were, her daughter's sexuality, robbing her child of anything resembling sexual autonomy. For this reason, the everyday lyrics and rhythms of daily, domestic enslavement—to the state, one's parents, and standard forms of growth—appear in the vibrant writing of Precious, in the signifiers I have here selected:

> I was left back when I was twelve because I had a baby for my fahver.
>   (Sapphire 1997: 3)
> I ain' did nothin'! (Ibid.)
> I disappears from the day. (Ibid.: 18)
> I see me, first grade, pink dress dirty sperms stuffs on it. (Ibid.)
> Mama's hand creepy spider, up my legs, in my pussy. (Ibid.: 21)
> Ize gone. (Ibid.)
> First he mess up my life fucking me, then he mess up the fucking talkin'.
>   (Ibid.: 24)
> My twat jumping juicy, it feel good. I feel shamed. (Ibid.)
> Carl come over fuck us'es. (Ibid.: 35)
> Sometimes fuck feel good. That confuse me, everything get swimming.
>   (Ibid.)
> But something like birds . . . fly through my heart. (Ibid.: 40)
> Weze ignerent. (Ibid.: 42)
> Farrakhan say . . . problem is not crack but the cracker! I go for that shit.
>   (Ibid.: 83)

Come in 8:55 a.m., sit down, don't move till the bell ring to go home. I wet
   myself. Don't know why I don't get up, but I don't. I jus' sit there and
   pee. (Ibid.: 37)
I wonder what reading books be like. (Ibid.: 51)
I feel panicking panicking—I don't know alphabetical order—whas that!
   (Ibid.)
prblm not jus HIV it mama Dady . . . I escap dem like Harriet [Tubman].
   (Ibid.: 101)
Mama give me orders, Daddy porno talk me, school never did learn me.
   (Ibid.: 62)
But then I feel the hot sauce hot cha cha feeling when he be fucking me.
   (Ibid.: 58)
feel like killing Mama. But I don't, instead I call little Precious and say,
   Come to Mama but I means me. (Ibid.: 59)
something stuck in me, growing in me, making me bigger. (Ibid.: 62)
I think my mind a TV set smell like between my muver's legs. (Ibid.: 57)

Crucially, this voice does not voice innocence, even bruised innocence. The
expected phrase, "First he mess up my life fucking me," is followed by a phrase
you would never have guessed—"then he mess up the fucking talkin'"—making
for a tonal stack in a single line. This is not the sound of vanquished sexuality:
girl as only eternally damaged sexual goods.[33] True, certain signifiers seem to
connote confusion, disappearance, shame, and roiling dislocation. And there is
uncompromising, unprettifying metaphorical trackings of a mental struggle in the
oddly conceptual line: "I think my mind a TV set smell like between my muver's
legs." But there is also a bold refrain of sexual response (the "hot cha cha feeling")—god knows in all its problematic mix, moving in and out of a longing for a
boyfriend ("fucking a cute boy, I think about that")—running alongside a passion
for the alphabet ("whas that!"). Surely, you can see sexual abuse sticking to these
signifiers: what she describes. And you can clearly perceive state neglect sticking to them, too, in the literacy level they depict. These twin stickings—abuse
stuck to signifiers to which stick signs of state neglect—is how the match is made
between state abuse and domestic abuse of children's libidos and attachments. But
throughout the novel, especially by the end, the Precious signifiers also connote
such libidinal longing for signification. Some surprising version of the "hot cha
cha feeling" shows up in her passion for reading, for learning how meanings wind
themselves around the (arbitrary) signifiers that make up the alphabet.[34] And the

undeniably pleasurable but confusing ecstasy of sexual orgasm seems to slide over the ecstasy of letters, becoming not fully distinguishable from them.

Push, that is, refuses to separate the sediments of its tonal stacks, its "vertical din" (Barthes 1974: 12). It will not let you desexualize Precious by assigning her sexualization only to outside forces, her parents most of all. Nor will it allow you to sexualize her along one plane, solely through abuse. Book-length, then, this depicted longing for sexual autonomy wed to literacy comes out on paper as a form of latency: the temporal, tonal stutter of something stuck in her, growing in her, making her bigger, as she becomes a pyramid of tones that grows and expands across the page. Even more fascinating is the fact that only much deeper in the novel do we get to see what her push toward writing first looked like, in its most latent, inchoate state. Here are some of her first written lines, looking like poems, her teacher's translations running beneath them (her lesbian teacher, named Blu Rain, is helping her push):

li Mg o mi m
(*Little Mongo on my mind*)
Litte mony is mi cie
(*Little Mongo is my child*)

A is fr Afrc
　　　(*for Africa*)
B is for u bae
　　　(*you baby*)
C is cl w bk
　　　(*colored we black*)
D is dog
E is el l/m
　　　(*evil like mama*)
F is Fuck

Ms Rain
Mi an Abdul got a scrit
(*Me and Abdul got a secret*)
I tell yo latr promois
(*I tell you later promise*)
no i tell yo now
IV HIV HIV U an Mi coold hav HIV

(IV HIV HIV You and me could have HIV)
mi sun God Allh
(my son God Allah)
Alice Walk pra o IV VI YWXYZ
(Alice Walker pray oh IV VI YWXYZ)
I ah V I I H IH I HIV
HIV.
Precious P. Jones

The effect is a strong pull back to the signifier, making sonic force bizarrely for the eye—at least for the reader, for whom these signifiers make tongue puzzles the eye and mind can grasp as written sounds making sense to Precious, since she possesses these sounds in her head, despite their alien appearance to the reader, and despite the fact that Precious is a manifest latency as a stack of words. What results, perhaps, is the making of a kind of language poetry out of a girl's attempts to mean and have her meanings seen, meanings that revolve around her baby from her father (a baby who's her brother, in a kinship growing sideways). Expression here *is* an experiment: a poet's concocting experimental poems out of written sounds of longings to express. And another concept grandly emerges. Just as Precious is gaining ground and entering into a progress narrative—she has had her baby and won an award for her literacy—Precious discovers she's HIV positive (her father's died of AIDS).

HIV is a bold plot turn, a signifying stutter around three letters (just three letters, HIV), and an authorial kick in the heart. You don't see it coming. When it comes in the film, at the point you and Precious hear her mother say it, the screen breaks into fantasy, dissociation, and swelling sonic pulse. The music amps to a vibrancy almost threatening to your ears, and Precious appears in fluorescent colors as she auditions to play the part of . . . Precious. Here we have a scene wedding viewers' "heartbreak" to a girl's assertive, in-your-face representation of herself to herself. True, at this point in book and film, HIV washes like a wave over everything, over every aspect of the story, back and forth, swamping any sense of assured growing "up" you'd assigned to Precious, knocking her narrative onto its side.

But then you realize something. Powerfully, you recognize, these texts depict that Precious's swing into her latent talent for poetry has temporally coincided with her HIV—with her knock sideways into her life of lyrical nows. Moreover, the novel ("written" by Precious in her own "voice") has perhaps been told from this position. Maybe the perceptions we receive *as* Precious—fresh, lubricated, granular, vibrant—should be seen as soaking in the letters HIV (which stand for latency), making what we "hear" triply rare: the imagined voice of latent sexuality, sideways growth, and the ambitious-but-tipping-sideways futurity that the character Beloved could only largely point to through poetic silence.

Precious, importantly, is something less ethereal but no less conceptual than the ghost Beloved. Precious is beloved as a dormancy we hear. For those with ears to hear an idea.

Coda: Spectating Lyrical Fat

Concluding, let me clarify the agency issue central to this essay. The world documentaries could have respected children's passion for signification by engaging children as a signifying force, letting them speak in a range of ways on the tricky, sexualized topics at hand (as *War Dance* does, *War Dance* can, because its topic is war, not sex). Those real bodies could demonstrate their agency if the filmmakers would simply go there. Sadly, they don't. *Push* goes there, but the voice of the child is Sapphire's fiction—and an experimental voice, to boot. All of which amounts to an agency quandary, leaving us to choose between loquacious-but-conceptual fictional children (as in *Push*) and documented children with faces that block us. I've tried to indicate why I choose the former over the latter, why I champion fiction's children, in this context. Where does *Precious* fall inside my preference?

Come back to the eye. Here, at the end, return for a moment to what strikes the eye in the film *Precious*: one child's fat.[35] Does fat congeal the face in the way that cliché stops up the face, stops the viewer at the face, in the documentaries I have discussed? Even more strangely, does a girl's fat make her forceful dormancy somehow hard to hear? Or does fat *convey* it?

As I have suggested, there is a problem when manifest latency turns into image on the cinema screen. Something stops moving, stops at the face. In the documentaries, outside of *War Dance*, this facial barrier has no fertile backside. There's no luminous back-of-the-face to this face on my back. This clichéd image constitutes a child, in a standard way, but sends the viewer running from a child who asks too much. Or perhaps it bores us: it's a frigid face in its frozen form. It does not seduce. This is what the philosopher Emmanuel Levinas (1969) doesn't explore in his ethics of the face—and what Judith Butler (2004: 135), engaging Levinas, understandably doesn't get to either, as both explore whether the face "bespeaks a divine prohibition against killing." She says cool things (of course, she's Judith Butler): she claims the face can't really speak; the face is not reducible either to the mouth or to what it utters; so one would need to hear the face as it speaks in something other than language (132–34).

I like these thoughts enormously. But I'm not sure there's obligation at the face. We may run from a face in "self-defense"—claiming something like reverse pedophilia, as I've shown. Thus we need a queerer ethics of the face, where the question becomes: Is there a seduction, a scene of desire we enter into? Do we take the bait to find the *story* of the face? Might we hear the face through language that lures us into a latency inside faciality? Do we agree, analyst-style, to take on this suffering? Remember, Lacan says the analyst suffers a Passion in analysis.[36] We must be seduced . . . by a face . . . on the move. . . .

Which takes us to fat, which is where I end. What in the world can the film *Precious* possibly accomplish, given that two indispensable features of the novel disappear: Precious's poems and (her rendering of) sexual longing?[37] How can this film do anything but fail, given these holes? When I saw the film, I was riveted to a facial drowning. Precious's face seemed to be submerged, seemed to have sunk under the waves of abuse rolling over her. Her voice seemed thrown down a well behind her face so that her face rarely seemed to be talking. Instead, what spoke was Precious's fat. Her face was displaced to the space of her fat. And something enormously telling moved me there, making me hold her facial drowning in tandem with her redolent plumpness.

That was my hunch. And I who was seduced by the-face-displaced have by now followed it into its slipstream of manifest latency. I *could* show, given time and space, via sharp dissection, that the poems' tones (from the novel *Push*) are hiding in the fat (from the film *Precious*), making for strangely *lyrical* fat. Fascinating sets of repeating elements in this film move in and out of adipose tissue, making for a set of accumulated tones—a tonal stack—but here through sight, layering, playing against the worn notion of personal expression so as to "voice" what is on the move; what is latent now. Balled together here are contentious connotations of physical power and invisibility; a bodily fortress that is a prison, open to invasions by rape and grease (a strange invasive pair), all stacking tones of anger, loneliness, muffled longing, mumbled protest, and a kind of hope-buried-under-outgrowths that *like fat* signal hidden folds and a buildup over time. There are remarkable syntagmatic chains to be found in single scenes, revealing how associations slide sideways on the back of fat, tying poverty to matters of literacy, sexuality, state neglect, and child abuse. I could show you.

Maybe you, too, have sensed these effects? My claiming that I might be one of few viewers to read the film this way is meant to honor the many fine critics, students, and friends who have said that they just can't stomach this film. I am merely showing how the film *could* be read—indeed, how I read it—if one dissects it very slowly and to an extent that many viewers won't, given the constraints on their time and desire. Hence it is simply a matter of speed, not any cleverness, that lends a certain, more palatable reading of *Precious* for me. But who cares? The fat falls flat for so many viewers. The weight of the history of depictions of African American women, for so many spectators, crushes micro-visual-textures that could be telling for the face in the fat.[38]

Hence, on this front of the palpable capture of latent sexuality, latent talent, latent meaning, latent virus, and even latent faciality, we need novels and their sonic properties—where we can thankfully see around, hear around, visualized children who block our sight.

Notes

Yesterday's tomorrow has become now. Fitting for this volume, this essay began as a keynote for a conference at Bowdoin College in April 2010, "Tomorrow's Parties: A Queer Americanist Colloquium," organized and orchestrated by the incomparable Pete Coviello. Indeed, a string of yesterdays, since that time, has nurtured this essay. I specifically want to acknowledge my smart and passionate seminar participants from the summer of 2011 at the School of Criticism and Theory at Cornell University, where I led a seminar, "Sexuality and Childhood in a Global Frame: Queer Theory and Beyond." That summer's engagements dramatically shaped the thoughts I offer here. And these stimulations followed with many remarkable audiences, including those at Monash University Prato Center in Prato, Italy, UC Berkeley, Tulane University, University of Texas Law School, UCLA, University of Minnesota, University of Alberta, University of Utah (Tanner Humanities Center and the Law School), University of Wisconsin–Milwaukee, Emory University, Indiana University, Aarhus University in Denmark, and the University of London, Goldsmiths College. Warmest thanks as always to the wizard kt farley, whose technical support has been inestimable.

1. See, e.g., Denizet-Lewis 2009; Hoffman 2011; Rosin 2008; Amar (this issue); Gill-Peterson 2014.

2. Though it covered a number of texts from the twenty-first century, my book *The Queer Child, or Growing Sideways in the Twentieth Century* (2009) largely focused on dynamics in the 1900s, and quite principally in the 1990s. Hence, it is clearly time to theorize the queer child again, and anew. For discussion of the categories I proceed to mention—children queered by money, gender, sexuality, race, ghostly gayness, and imagined innocence—see my introduction from *The Queer Child*, "Growing Sideways, or Why Children Appear to Get Queerer in the Twentieth Century."

3. This latter emphasis on children's slipping to the side of this fantasy constitutes a

major difference between my work on the queer child and the significant, forceful focus of Lee Edelman's *No Future: Queer Theory and the Death Drive* (2004). As you will recall, in *No Future*, Edelman criticized the figure of the Child (capitalized to underscore its force and singularity) as a pleasure-killing conception of frightful, brutish normativity. I took a different path to critique. That is, I opened the *queerness* of children into complication, unseen possibility, radical darkness (not normativity), and queer innocence of all things. Moreover, I did so via fiction as the only dense archive I could draw on, given the strictures on research on children and the dearth of histories of sexual childhood.

4.   To put these matters differently, I do not intend to be flip or breezy in my presentation. My speed and shortened tone are meant to perform two things at once: move quickly where I can through points I have established in *The Queer Child* and others have established in their illuminating work on childhood; and offer formulations and even brief readings that certainly I, and perhaps others (should I be so lucky), will unpack in future essays.

5.   Keep in mind, of course, that the suburbs are themselves defying our old stereotypes of suburban-driven anything, at least in some regions of our country. For an excellent study on this front, see Tongson 2011.

6.   For exact definitions of *latency*, read on. I delay them for the moment.

7.   I say "again" because this cry has been both cyclical and, in the twentieth century, perpetual. For a crucial essay that gives historical texture to denials of child sexuality—especially their intensification—beginning in the 1980s, see Angelides 2004. The classic lament over children's disappearance remains, of course, Postman 1982. By contrast, queer theory has generated questions about the idea of the sexual child: matters involving children's protogayness, animal appetites, temporal strangeness, attention from pedophiles, and links to the death drive. In addition to *The Queer Child*, see also Sedgwick 1993, 154–64; Moon 1998; Kincaid 1998; Bruhm and Hurley 2004; Edelman 2004.

8.   Readers will have to read my book for how the "trans child" fits into this argument. Certainly, as I argue there, transgendered children and gender-queer children have been subjected to harmful delays of unspeakable sorts—by parents, medical and psychiatric authorities, and public discourse. The distinction of the ghostly gay child, and why it *figures* childhood delay, is its insistent and quite intense *sexualization* by authoritative forces and its own sexual self-understandings. The sexual assumptions surrounding "gay" slide onto the "gay" child *as a concept* and thus have made its present-tense existence so precarious (since these assumptions are deemed so "adult"). Trans kids get sexualized in various ways, but often their sexual object choice is actually downplayed (harmfully, prejudicially)—even by allies—so as to focus on gender identity. The complex collision between "trans" and "gay" for many queer kids is beyond the scope of this present essay, though my current research takes

it as a focus. For a discussion of all these issues, especially for a nonessentializing view of the queer child—arguing gay children are not born gay but, in complicated ways, relate to the signifier gay—see Stockton 2009.

9. As I was sending this essay to reviewers, the National Coalition for Lesbian Rights was running its Born Perfect campaign. A sophisticated summary, critique, and discussion of the It Gets Better campaign can be found in Mason 2012.

10. Growing public belief in gay children (or largely teens?) seems to have forced the Boy Scouts' hand, though their split decision until just recently—gay kids allowed, adult gay scoutmasters still unwelcome—indicates a less than full embrace of gays.

11. Quite unsurprisingly, when worry over kids' "getting" sexualized is voiced, girls are the overwhelming focus of discussion.

12. According to Geralyn White Dreyfous (2012), executive producer of *The Day My God Died* (2003) and *Born into Brothels* (2004), this genre began around 2000 in the United States.

13. Jacques Derrida's sense of latency is wedded to his notion of delay as the ineluctable effect of our reading along a chain of words (in a sentence, for example), where meaning is delayed, deferred, always latent because we read in sequence, go forward in a sentence, not yet knowing what words are ahead of us, while we must take the words we have passed *with* us as we go, making meaning wide and hung in suspense. See Derrida 1986.

14. For my theories on these libidinal attachments to the signifier, see Stockton 2015a and 2015b.

15. For my detailed discussions of the place of black children in the discourse of US childhood, and for my tremendous debt in my thinking to fictions by African American writers, see Stockton 2006, especially chapters 2, 4, and 5; and Stockton 2009, especially chapter 5, introduction, and conclusion.

16. When I wrote this part of this essay in early 2010, there were only film reviews of *Precious*—not academic articles. Despite the surprising commercial success of this indie film, and its acclaim at Sundance, the Golden Globes, and the Oscars, attacks on the film were numerous and scathing. See, e.g., Reed 2010; White 2009; Downs 2009; Marble 2009. Since that time, a good deal of commentary by academics has emerged. Though none of it existed to help me at the point of this essay's composition, it should interest readers to see where it has gone. Most important, an issue of the journal *Black Camera* (2012) focused on the film, in and around *Push*, the novel from which the film is drawn. Perhaps unsurprisingly, this issue overwhelmingly sees the film as doing significant intellectual and political work. Also overwhelmingly, the essays in this issue take a dialectical, doubled view of this film's politics. David Wall (2012: 220) puts the matter this way: "Is [the film] an excoriating indictment of a society in which a black underclass is left to rot? Or is it merely one more predictable iteration of the pathology of the black family that panders to white liberal sensibilities?

It is, of course, both and more." Suzette Spencer (2012: 66–67) adds: "The essays and commentaries here do not discount the negative power of racist and homophobic gazes. Nor do they discount or ignore the potential for black cultural production to become consumed into vectors of denigrating stereotypes. . . . the hope is that this Close-Up will inspire ways of rethinking the ethical stakes of projects like *Precious* and *Push* in the contemporary moment." See also Kanagawa 2012; Mask 2012; Crawford 2012; Edwards 2012; and, in a different journal, Jarman 2012.

17. No other critic who addresses *Push* and *Precious* takes this tack. In fact, the *sexual* agency of Precious is barely acknowledged and largely unexplored. Nonetheless, the reader should consult two important chapters in books that in part address *Push*, each worthy on its own terms: Harkins 2009: 216–24; and Doane and Hodges 2001: 124–31.

18. This phrase "teen/child" is crucial to my argument. Precious Jones is not a tween in the novel's present—she is sixteen, although she is twelve when she first gets pregnant— but she is alternately seen as a child and teen throughout the text. In the novel, Precious states: "She quiet, quiet. Say, 'Shame, thas a shame. Twelve years old, twelve years old. . . . Was you ever, I mean did you ever get to be a chile?' Thas a stupid question, did I ever get to be a chile? I *am* a chile" (Sapphire 1997: 12–13).

19. I haven't found an essay that takes this approach. Other critics who address the novel or film do not speak of signifiers, the latency of signification, or sexual childhood, much less link these three domains.

20. Several essays address the novel's experimental nature, with its impressive collection of forms (letters, journal, slave narrative, poems), but not the character herself as a concept, as *in herself* an experimental form. In this respect, the novel could surprisingly be read as fitting and fulfilling many of the notions discussed in Dworkin and Goldsmith 2011. By contrast, many essays convey the sense of Katie Kanagawa's claim (2012: 117) that Precious gradually "cultivates her voice," gaining what Spencer (2012: 58) says is a "personal mode of insight." See also Jarman 2012: 177; Crawford 2012: 193–94, 196, 200; Muller 2013: 2, 6, 9.

21. Throughout this essay, I often use the obviously politically incorrect phrase "the HIV child" instead of "children with HIV" so as to underscore the phantasmic aspects of children infected with the virus.

22. And it should be noted that we are entering new terrain with HIV with the arrival of Truvada: the treatment drug now being used for pre-exposure prophylaxis (PrEP) by gay men. For further reading, see Juzwiak 2014 and Glazek 2013.

23. For highly different approaches from mine to the novel's focus on HIV, consult Watkins-Hayes, Patterson, and Armour 2011, along with Highberg 2010.

24. Deemed a threat to public health, he was expelled from middle school in the state of Indiana, even though doctors clearly stated he posed no risk to other students. Even when allowed to return to school, he found himself opposed by parents and teachers who found his presence threatening.

25. In *The Queer Child* (Stockton 2009), I made these points from a theoretical and literary standpoint. Thankfully, now we have Robin Bernstein's remarkable confirmation of these claims, via her impeccable *Racial Innocence* (2011).

26. In my opinion, two realms remain fairly undertheorized in queer theory: the queering force of race in Anglo-American texts on children; and, quite substantially, global problems and depictions of childhood, especially as they touch on HIV, poverty, youth protest, children's street life, sexual trafficking, and child soldiering. Such foci may allow us, through the lens of childhood, to scout the overlapping and contentious borders among queer theory, critical race theory, and postcolonial theorizations, as we specifically put under pressure Sigmund Freud's notion of *Nachtraglichkeit*, Derrida's stress on delay, Gayatri Spivak's take on the subaltern, Edward Said's idea of Orientalism, and Lacan's delineations among (what he names) need/demand/desire. On the first front of the queering force of race in US childhood, see Stockton 2009, the introduction, chapter 5, and the conclusion; see also parts of both Eng 2001 and Eng 2010. On the second front, there has been much work outside queer theory. See, e.g., Katz 2005; Goddard et al. 2005; James and Prout 1990; Cooter 1992; Burman 1996; Castaneda 2002; Wells 2009; Burman 2008; Burman and Stacey 2010.

27. My specific stress—how these effects affect the idea of the sexual child—is my unique contribution, I hope, to the voluminous, excellent array of studies on the long history of representing "third world" bodies (often children) in a range of media. These fine studies do not see the images of third world children as playing a *funkified role* in how US general culture navigates the problem of child sexuality. It is the speculative connections I make among kid Orientalism, reverse pedophilia, and manifest latency (my new concepts) that are my offering. For important samples of other scholars' work, see Moeller 1999; Sarat, Basler, and Dumm 2011; Chouliaraki 2006; Cartwright 2008; Mirzoeff 2011.

28. Though I drop the quotation marks from here, you can consider the word *Western*—along with the terms *Eastern*, *the Orient*, and *the Occident*—to be used under erasure.

29. Clearly, I am claiming, the means by which we make the Child whom Lee Edelman (2004) discusses in *No Future* have become serpentine—much more complex now than when Edelman wrote *No Future*.

30. For his discussion of these terms, see Lacan 1982: 80–83.

31. See Stockton 2006: 177–203.

32. In *Push*, Precious is shown reading Alice Walker's novel *The Color Purple*. For this reason, and quite logically, almost to a person, critics discuss *The Color Purple* as the film's and novel's most relevant touchstone. See, e.g., Spencer 2012: 55, 70; Kanagawa 2012: 124; Jarman 2012: 179; Mask 2012: 96; and Edwards 2012: 74–76. But clearly I am saying that Morrison's *Beloved* is the more stunning intertext for the novel *Push*. Even so, Riché Richardson (2012: 176) views *Beloved's* relevance (the film's, not the novel's) in terms of its depiction of "the long history of violence against the black mater-

nal body." To be sure, I agree, but I want to suggest that a nest of issues—daughter versus mother, sexual childhood, and memory-as-infection—is situated here.

33. For another instance, to put it mildly, where an author turns up the dial on agency and harm simultaneously, readers should revisit Nabokov 1997. See my discussion of that duality in my chapter "What Drives the Sexual Child? Mysterious Motions of Children's Motives," in Stockton 2009: 119–53.

34. Consider these comments my reply to Barbara Bush's tamer view that "learning to read can change someone's life"—comments she made in response to *Precious* ("Barbara Bush Sees Promise in 'Precious'" 2009).

35. For two quite different takes on fat—quite different from mine—that even so may complement what I offer here, see Jarman 2012 and Muller 2013. Focusing on the physical form of the actress Gabourey Sidibe, who portrays Precious, Jarman (2012: 168) writes: "Sidibe's nonnormative body is often situated as the primary problem of the film. For example, critical fixation on her excess weight trumps the abuse, literacy, and economic issues faced by the protagonist in Engber's (2009) essay for *Slate* titled, tellingly, 'How Did Precious Get So Fat?' [and here Jarman quotes Engber]: 'Lee Daniels's *Precious* provides a hellish tableau of petty theft, physical abuse, attempted infanticide, rape, incest, . . . welfare fraud, HIV/AIDS, homophobia, school violence, teen pregnancy, self-hatred, and illiteracy. But the most arresting figure of urban poverty is the one that lumbers through nearly every frame: The 300-pound Gabby Sidibe.'" Jarman then comments: "Critics resist racial stereotypes by rejecting the body of Sidibe; in effect, however, their comments reinforce intensely negative stereotypes about large bodies and remobilize some of the very elements of objectification and dehumanization that the film sets out to condemn" (169).

36. See Schneiderman 1983: 113–14.

37. Precious, in the film, imagines herself with a light-skinned boyfriend, but this tame fantasy carries none of the sexual force of her arresting statements of desire in *Push*.

38. This is my version of the dialectical, doubled view of the film's politics that I discuss in note 16. Also, for a wonderful new intervention in black feminist interpretive practice, one in accord with my earlier writings in *Beautiful Bottom, Beautiful Shame: Where "Black" Meets "Queer,"* see Nash 2014.

References

Amar, Paul. 2016. "The Street, the Sponge, and the Ultra: Queer Logics of Children's Rebellion and Political Infantilization." *GLQ* 22, no. 4.

Angelides, Steven. 2004. "Feminism, Child Sexual Abuse, and the Erasure of Child Sexuality." *GLQ* 10, no. 2: 141–77.

"Barbara Bush Sees Promise in 'Precious.'" 2009. *NPR*, December 11. www.npr.org /templates/story/story.php?storyId=121335962.

Barthes, Roland. 1974. *The Pleasure of the Text*. Translated by Richard Miller. New York: Macmillan.

Bernstein, Robin. 2011. *Racial Innocence: Performing American Childhood from Slavery to Civil Rights*. New York: New York University Press.

Born into Brothels. 2004. DVD. Directed by Ross Kauffman and Zana Briski. New York: Image/Thinkfilms.

Bruhm, Steven, and Natasha Hurley, eds. 2004. *Curiouser: On the Queerness of Children*. Minneapolis: University of Minnesota Press.

Burman, Erica. 1996. "Local, Global, or Globalized: Child Development and International Child Rights Legislation." *Childhood: A Global Journal of Child Research* 3, no. 1: 45–66.

Burman, Erica. 2008. *Developments: Child, Image, Nation*. New York: Routledge.

Burman, Erica, and Jackie Stacey. 2010. "The Child and Childhood in Feminist Theory." *Feminist Theory* 11, no. 3: 227–40.

Butler, Judith. 2004. *Precarious Life: The Powers of Mourning and Violence*. London: Verso.

Cartwright, Lisa. 2008. *Moral Spectatorship: Technologies of Voice and Affect in Postwar Representations of the Child*. Durham, NC: Duke University Press.

Castaneda, Claudia. 2002. *Figurations: Child, Bodies, World*. Durham, NC: Duke University Press.

Chouliaraki, Lilie. 2006. *The Spectatorship of Suffering*. London: Sage.

Cooter, Roger. 1992. *In the Name of the Child*. London: Routledge.

Crawford, Margo Natalie. 2012. "The Counterliteracy of Postmelancholy." *Black Camera: An International Film Journal* 4, no. 1: 192–209.

Denizet-Lewis, Benoit. 2009. "Coming Out in Middle School." *New York Times Magazine*, September 23.

Derrida, Jacques. 1986. "Différance." In *Deconstruction in Context*, edited by Mark C. Taylor, 396–420. Chicago: University of Chicago Press.

Doane, Janice, and Devon Hodges. 2001. *Telling Incest: Narratives of Dangerous Remembering from Stein to Sapphire*. Ann Arbor: University of Michigan Press.

Downs, Jim. 2009. "Are We All Precious?" *Chronicle of Higher Education*, December 13.

Dreyfous, Geralyn White. 2012. Remarks at screening, April, Salt Lake City, Utah.

Dworkin, Craig, and Kenneth Goldsmith, eds. 2011. *Against Expression: An Anthology of Conceptual Writing*. Evanston, IL: Northwestern University Press.

Edelman, Lee. 2004. *No Future: Queer Theory and the Death Drive*. Durham, NC: Duke University Press.

Edwards, Erica R. 2012. "Turning into Precious: The Black Women's Empowerment Adaptation and the Interruptions of the Absurd." *Black Camera: An International Film Journal* 4, no. 1: 74–95.

Eng, David. 2001. *Racial Castration*. Durham, NC: Duke University Press.

Eng, David. 2010. *The Feeling of Kinship: Queer Liberalism and the Racialization of Intimacy*. Durham, NC: Duke University Press.

Engber, Daniel. 2012. "How Did Precious Get So Fat?" *Slate*, November 12. www.slate
.com/blogs/browbeat/2009/11/12/how_did_precious_get_so_fat.html.

Flint, F. S. 1913. "Imagisme." *Poetry* 1: 198–200.

Gill-Peterson, Julian. 2014. "The Value of the Future: The Child Entrepreneur and the
Neoliberal Labor of Race." Paper presented at the annual meeting of the Cultural
Studies Association, Salt Lake City, Utah, May 30.

Glazek, Christopher. 2013. "Why Is No One on the First Treatment to Prevent H.I.V?"
New Yorker, September 30.

Goddard, Jim, et al., eds. 2005. *The Politics of Childhood: International Perspectives,
Contemporary Developments.* Basingstoke, UK: Palgrave.

Harkins, Gillian. 2009. *Everybody's Family Romance: Reading Incest in Neoliberal America.* Minneapolis: University of Minnesota Press.

Highberg, Nels P. 2010. "The (Missing) Faces of African American Girls with AIDS."
Feminist Formations 22, no. 1: 1–20.

Hoffman, Jan. 2011. "A Girl's Nude Photo, and Altered Lives: When Texting Turns
Explicit at Fourteen, Repercussions Last." *New York Times*, March 26.

I Am Because We Are. 2008. DVD. Directed by Nathan Rissman. New York: Virgil Films.

James, Allison, and Alan Prout, eds. 1990. *Constructing and Reconstructing Childhood:
Contemporary Issues in the Sociological Study of Childhood.* Basingstoke, UK:
Falmer.

Jarman, Michelle. 2012. "Cultural Consumption and Rejection of Precious Jones: Pushing
Disability into the Discussion of Sapphire's *Push* and Lee Daniels's *Precious*." *Feminist Formations* 24, no. 2: 163–85.

Jones, Abigail. 2014. "Sex and the Single Tween." *Newsweek*, January 22. mag.newsweek
.com/2014/01/24/sex-single-tween.html.

Juzwiak, Rich. 2014. "What Is Safe Sex? The Raw and Uncomfortable Truth about
Truvada." March 4. gawker.com/what-is-safe-sex-the-raw-and-uncomfortable
-truth-about-1535583252.

Kaiser, Jon D. 1993. *Immune Power: A Comprehensive Healing Program for HIV.* New
York: St. Martin's.

Kanagawa, Katie M. 2012. "Dialectical Mediation: The Play of Fantasy and Reality in
Precious." *Black Camera: An International Film Journal* 4, no. 1: 117–38.

Katz, Cindi. 2005. *Growing Up Global: Economic Restructuring and Children's Everyday
Lives.* Minneapolis: University of Minnesota Press.

Kenner, Hugh. 1983. "William Carlos Williams's Rhythm of Ideas." *New York Times*,
September 18. www.nytimes.com/1983/09/18/books/william-carlos-williams
-s-rhythm-of-ideas.html?pagewanted=all&pagewanted=print.

Kincaid, James R. 1998. *Erotic Innocence: The Culture of Child Molesting.* Durham, NC:
Duke University Press.

Lacan, Jacques. 1982. *Feminine Sexuality: Jacques Lacan and the École freudienne.*
Translated by Jacqueline Rose. New York: Palgrave.

Levinas, Emmanuel. 1969. *Totality and Infinity: An Essay on Exteriority.* Translated by
  Alphonso Lingis. Pittsburgh: Duquesne University Press.

Lispector, Clarice. 1992. *The Hour of the Star.* Translated by Giovanni Pontiero. New
  York: New Directions.

Marble, Justin. 2009. "Not So 'Precious.'" *ArtsFuse*, November 26.

Mask, Mia. 2012. "The Precarious Politics of *Precious*: A Close Reading of a Cinematic
  Text." *Black Camera: An International Film Journal* 4, no. 1: 96–116.

Mason, Derritt. 2012. "On Children's Literature and the (Im)Possibility of It Gets Better."
  ESC: English Studies in Canada 38, nos. 3–4: 83–104.

Mirzoeff, Nicholas. 2011. *The Right to Look: A Counterhistory of Visuality.* Durham, NC:
  Duke University Press.

Moeller, Susan D. 1999. *Compassion Fatigue: How the Media Sell Disease, Famine, War,
  and Death.* New York: Routledge.

Moon, Michael. 1998. *A Small Boy and Others: Imitation and Initiation in American Culture.* Durham, NC: Duke University Press.

Morrison, Toni. 1987. *Beloved.* New York: Plume.

Muller, Claudia. 2013. "The Welfare Mother and the Fat Poor: Stereotypical Images
  and the Success Narrative in Sapphire's *Push*." *COPAS: Current Objectives of Post-
  graduate American Studies* 14, no. 1. copas.uni-regensburg.de/article/view/162.

Nabokov, Vladimir. 1997. *Lolita.* New York: Vintage.

Nash, Jennifer C. 2014. *The Black Body in Ecstasy: Reading Race, Reading Pornography.*
  Durham, NC: Duke University Press.

Navarro, Mireya. 1993. "Growing Up in the Shadow of the AIDS Virus." *New York Times*,
  March 21.

Newcombe, Alyssa, Ron Claiborne, and Nancy Ramsey. 2011. "HIV-Positive Boy Talks
  of Being Denied Entry to Hershey School." *ABC News*, December 2. abcnews.go
  .com/US/hiv-positive-student-discusses-denial-admissions-hershey-school/story
  ?id=15074075.

Postman, Neil. 1982. *The Disappearance of Childhood.* New York: Vintage.

Pound, Ezra. 1934. *ABC of Reading.* New York: New Directions.

Precious. 2009. DVD. Directed by Lee Daniels. Santa Monica, CA: Lionsgate.

Reed, Ishmael. 2010. "Fade to White." *New York Times*, February 5.

Richardson, Lynda. 1999. "Born with H.I.V., Struggling with Teen-Age Lives." *New
  York Times*, April 18. www.nytimes.com/1990/04/18/nyregion/born-with-hiv
  -struggling-with-teen-age-lives.html?pagewanted=all.

Richardson, Riché. 2012. "*Push*, *Precious*, and New Narratives of Slavery in Harlem."
  Black Camera: An International Film Journal 4, no. 1: 161–80.

Rosin, Hanna. 2008. "A Boy's Life." *Atlantic Magazine*, November.

Said, Edward W. 1979. *Orientalism.* New York: Vintage.

Sapphire. 1997. *Push.* New York: Vintage.

Sarat, Austin, Carleen R. Basler, and Thomas L. Dumm, eds. 2011. *Performances of Violence*. Amherst: University of Massachusetts Press.

Schneiderman, Stuart. 1983. *Jacques Lacan: The Death of an Intellectual Hero*. Cambridge, MA: Harvard University Press.

Sedgwick, Eve Kosofsky. 1993. "How to Bring Your Kids Up Gay: The War on Effeminate Boys." In *Tendencies*, 154–64. Durham, NC: Duke University Press.

Spencer, Suzette. 2012. "'They Look Way above Me, Put Me out of Their Eyes': Seeing the Subjects in *Precious*: An Introduction in Two Parts." *Black Camera: An International Film Journal* 4, no. 1: 66–67.

Stamm, Dan. 2011. "Hershey School Turns away Boy with HIV." *NBC Philadelphia*, November 30. www.nbcphiladelphia.com/news/health/Hershey-School-HIV-Lawsuit -Boy-134802368.html.

Stockton, Kathryn Bond. 2006. *Beautiful Bottom, Beautiful Shame: Where "Black" Meets "Queer."* Durham, NC: Duke University Press.

———. 2009. *The Queer Child, or Growing Sideways in the Twentieth Century*. Durham, NC: Duke University Press.

———. 2015a. "Reading as Kissing, Sex with Ideas: 'Lesbian' Barebacking?" *Los Angeles Review of Books*, March 8.

———. 2015b. "Surfacing (in the Heat of Reading): Is It Like Kissing or Some Other Sex Act?" *J19: The Journal of Nineteenth Century Americanists* 3, no. 1: 7–13. lareviewofbooks.org/essay/reading-kissing-sex-ideas-lesbian-barebacking.

Tongson, Karen. 2011. *Relocations: Queer Suburban Imaginaries*. New York: New York University Press.

Wall, David. 2012. "Close-Up Gallery: *Precious*." *Black Camera: An International Film Journal* 4, no. 1: 220.

War Dance. 2007. DVD. Directed by Sean Fine and Andrea Nix. New York: Velocity/ Thinkfilm.

Watkins-Hayes, Celeste, Courtney J. Patterson, and Amanda Armour. 2011. "*Precious*: Black Women, Neighborhood HIV/AIDS Risk, and Institutional Buffers." *Du Bois Review* 8, no. 1: 229–40.

Wells, Karen. 2009. *Childhood in a Global Perspective*. Cambridge, UK: Polity.

White, Armond. 2009. "Pride and Precious." *New York Press*, November 4.

SAME-SEX MARRIAGE LITIGATION AND CHILDREN'S RIGHT TO BE QUEER

Clifford Rosky

*T*his essay examines how lawyers and judges have framed the question of children's queerness in litigation over same-sex marriage. First, it argues that in *United States v. Windsor* and *Obergefell v. Hodges*, the US Supreme Court invoked the tropes of dignity, injury, and immutability to set the outer limits of sexual liberty for both children and adults. Next, the essay looks back to the early work of queer theorists, legal scholars, and lawyers to unearth a more promising vision of law's relationship to children's queerness. By juxtaposing how two judges approached the possibility of the gay child in Utah and California, it develops a claim that has yet to be vindicated—that the US Constitution protects every child's right to be queer.

Marriage Equality: The Indignity of Victory

Three years ago, in *United States v. Windsor*, the Supreme Court struck down the Defense of Marriage Act (DOMA), which defined the word *marriage* as "a legal union of one man and one woman" under federal law.[1] Last year, in *Obergefell v. Hodges*, the Court struck down the country's remaining state laws that prohibited same-sex couples from marrying and denied recognition to same-sex marriages performed in other states.[2] As a result of these rulings, the federal government now recognizes same-sex marriages and same-sex couples have the freedom to marry in all fifty states.

Needless to say, however, these rulings have not realized the most profound hopes and aspirations of the country's queers. To begin with, both rulings

GLQ 22:4
DOI 10.1215/10642684-3603090
© 2016 by Duke University Press

emphatically declare that the institution of marriage confers "dignity" upon couples who enter it. By doing so, they proudly privilege married over unmarried persons. In *Windsor*, the Court repeatedly speaks as if the dignity of human beings, and human relationships, was somehow derived from the government's authority to recognize marriages. In one passage, the Court claims that when the state of New York allowed same-sex couples to marry, "the State's decision to give this class of persons the right to marry conferred upon them a dignity and status of immense import" (2692). In another, the Court refers to "the equal dignity of same-sex marriages, a dignity conferred by the States in the exercise of their sovereign power" (2693). In yet another, the Court explains that the state's conferral of legal "responsibilities, as well as rights, enhance the dignity and integrity of the person" (2694). In the Court's view, DOMA was unconstitutional because it refused "to acknowledge a status the State finds to be dignified and proper" (2596).

In *Obergefell*, the Court could not plausibly claim that states like Ohio, Michigan, and Kentucky had "conferred dignity" on same-sex couples. Unlike New York, these states had specifically banned same-sex couples from marrying. Instead, the Court showers dignity on the institution of marriage and applauds the dignity of the petitioners for seeking to enter it. In just fifteen pages, the Court offers too many superlatives for marriage to present them in toto. The following paragraph, which purports "to note the history of the subject," is illustrative:

> From their beginning to their most recent page, the annals of history reveal the transcendent importance of marriage. The lifelong union of a man and a woman always has promised nobility and dignity to all persons, without regard to their station in life. Marriage is sacred to those who live by their religions and offers unique fulfillment to those who find meaning in the secular realm. Its dynamic allows two people to find a life that could not be found alone, for a marriage becomes greater than just the two persons. Rising from the most basic human needs, marriage is essential to our most profound hopes and aspirations. (2594)

Even after the opinion turns to legal analysis, the homage to marriage continues. Relying on "this Court's cases and the Nation's traditions," the Court posits that "marriage is a keystone of our social order"—"the foundation of the family and of society, without which there would be neither civilization nor progress" (2601). Quoting Alexis de Tocqueville, the Court posits that reverence for marriage is a defining feature of the nation itself: "There is certainly no country in the world where the tie of marriage is so much respected as in America" (2601). In light of the Court's earlier analysis in *Windsor*, it is hardly surprising that in *Obergefell*, the Court finds "dignity" in the decision of two persons to marry each other: "There is dignity in the bond between two men or two women who seek to marry and in their autonomy make such profound choices. . . . The right to marry thus dignifies couples who 'wish to define themselves by their commitment to each other'" (2599–2600).

Throughout the opinion, the Court praises the petitioners because they have shown such profound "respect" for the institution of marriage—like the Court, and the Nation itself: "It is the enduring importance of marriage that underlies the petitioners' contentions. This, they say, is their whole point. Far from seeking to devalue marriage, the petitioners seek it for themselves because of their respect—and need—for its privileges and responsibilities" (2594). "It would misunderstand these men and women to say they disrespect the idea of marriage. Their plea is that they do respect it, respect it so deeply that they seek to find its fulfillment for themselves" (2608).

By this point, the Court's spiral of dignification is almost too tight to trace: the Court dignifies marriage; marriage dignifies the petitioners; the petitioners dignify marriage; the Court dignifies the petitioners not only because marriage dignifies them, but also because they dignify marriage. . . .[3] Even so, one might hold out hope that the Court's effusive praise is little more than lofty rhetoric—what the lawyers call "dicta," rather than the reasoning or "holding" of the ruling itself.[4] But in a remarkable passage, the Court insists that the "respect" that the petitioners have shown for marriage is legally relevant and serves as a foundation of the constitutional claims that they have put forward: "*Were their intent to demean the revered idea and reality of marriage, the petitioners' claims would be of a different order.* But that is neither their purpose nor their submission" (2594; emphasis added).

The implication of such "submissions" is readily apparent: while granting same-sex couples the freedom to marry, the Court denigrates millions of unmarried persons and nonmarital relationships. To prove that marriage is "a two-person union unlike any other," the Court portrays unmarried people as lonely and fearful: "Marriage responds to the universal fear that a lonely person might call out only to find no one there" (2600). In the opinion's coda, this hierarchy of dignity and respect is made painfully clear. On the one hand, the Court writes, "No union is more profound than marriage, for it embodies the highest ideals of love, fidelity, devotion, sacrifice, and family" (2608). On the other hand, the Court notes that the petitioners' "hope is not to be condemned to live in loneliness, excluded from one of civilization's oldest institutions" (ibid.).

In expounding the importance of marriage, the Court emphasizes that the institution serves to promote children's best interests: "The right to marry . . . safeguards children and families and thus draws meaning from related rights of childrearing, procreation, and education" (2590). On several occasions, the Court observes, it has described the rights to marry, procreate, and parent "as a unified whole" (ibid.). Without the "recognition" that marriage affords, the Court reasons, "children suffer the stigma of knowing their families are somehow lesser" (ibid.). Although the Court insists that "the right to marry cannot be conditioned on the capacity or commitment to procreate" (ibid.), it indicates that marriage dignifies children as well as parents—and conversely that the responsibilities of procreation and parenting dignify the sexual relationship between two married adults.

Homophobia: The New Child Abuse

Of course, there is something ironic about the Court's invocation of procreation, parenting, and the protection of children in this particular context. For many years, opponents of same-sex marriage have insisted that procreation is the purpose of marriage, and same-sex couples cannot marry because they cannot procreate. More broadly, however, the question of children's welfare has long played a pivotal role in the LGBT movement's triumphs and setbacks. For a very long time, in a wide range of settings, public officials have justified discrimination against LGBT people by invoking what I have called "the fear of the queer child" (Rosky 2013: 607)— the premise that the state has a legitimate interest in promoting heteronormativity and discouraging queerness during childhood. The simplest version of this fear is that "exposure to homosexuality would turn children into homosexuals," but the idea is considerably more capacious, flexible, and nuanced than this simple formulation suggests.[5] In the broadest sense, it includes the fears that exposing children to homosexuality and gender variance will make them more likely to develop same-sex desires; engage in same-sex acts; form same-sex relationships; identify as lesbian, gay, bisexual, or transgender; or deviate from traditional gender roles.

Notwithstanding the LGBT movement's remarkable progress in recent years, examples of this fear are not hard to find. In *Windsor*, the opponents of same-sex marriage claimed that DOMA was justified by the government's interest in protecting children—specifically, in "promoting child-rearing by both a mother and a father."[6] Because of "the different challenges faced by boys and girls as they grow to adulthood," they reasoned, it was "at least rational to think that children benefit from having parental role models of both sexes" (ibid). As the term *role model* suggests, they implied that children would benefit from having both a mother and a father by learning the appropriate ways to be male or female, masculine or feminine, mother or father: "Men and women are different," they explained; "so are mothers and fathers" (ibid).

In the congressional debates over DOMA, the law's sponsors were less cryptic about the lessons that they sought to impart to "the children of America."[7] By posing a series of rhetorical questions, Representative Charles Canady signaled that the law was designed to channel children into heterosexual relationships:

> Should this Congress tell *the children of America* that it is a matter of indifference whether they establish families with a partner of the opposite sex or cohabit with someone of the same sex?
>
> Should this Congress tell *the children of America* that we as a society believe there is no moral difference between homosexual relationships and heterosexual relationships?
>
> Should this Congress tell *the children of America* that in the eyes of the law the parties to a homosexual union are entitled to all the rights and privileges that have always been reserved for a man and a woman united in marriage? (emphasis added)[8]

In a legislative report supporting the bill, Representative Canady cautioned his colleagues "against doing anything which might mislead *wavering children* into perceiving society as indifferent to the sexual orientation they develop," in order to protect society's interest "in reproducing itself" (emphasis added).[9]

In striking down DOMA, however, the *Windsor* Court found that the law was actually harming children, instead of protecting them. In addition to finding that DOMA "injured," "disparaged," and "demeaned" same-sex couples, the Court declared that the law "humiliates tens of thousands of children now being raised by same-sex couples" by making it "even more difficult for the children to understand the integrity and closeness of their own family and its concord with other families in their community and in their daily lives" (2695–96, 2594, 2595). As if that were not sufficient, the Court added that "DOMA also brings financial harm to children of same-sex couples" by raising "the cost of health care for families" and denying "benefits allowed to families upon the loss of a spouse and parent" (2596).

In *Obergefell*, the Court doubled down on the claim that laws against same-sex marriage are harmful to the children of same-sex couples: "Without the recognition, stability, and predictability marriage offers, these children suffer the stigma of knowing their families are somehow lesser. They also suffer the significant material costs of being raised by unmarried parents, relegated through no fault of their own to a more difficult and uncertain family life. The marriage laws at issue here thus harm and humiliate the children of same-sex couples" (2590). More than anything else, this paradigm shift signals the wholesale demise of discrimination against same-sex couples in family law. As Lauren Berlant (1997: 1, 5) reminds us, US citizenship and nationhood are perennially defined by reference to competing claims about children and childhood. As a result, Lee Edelman (2004: 3) adds, both sides of any legal or political conflict must be able to position themselves as "fighting for the children," because there is no other side for which one can fight. Once *Windsor* proclaimed that laws against same-sex marriage were "harming" and "humiliating" children—instead of benefiting or protecting them—it was just a matter of time until the movement won the freedom to marry and adopt in all fifty states.

This is good news for same-sex couples—or at least, for the "noble" and "dignified" couples who are willing and able to enter into the "sacred" union of spouses. But it is bad news for other sexual dissidents, whose lives are still routinely regulated in the name of protecting kids. If *Windsor* and *Obergefell* signal that such groups will not win the law's protection unless and until they can plausibly claim to be protecting children, then it may be a long time before sexual liberty comes to unmarried parents—not to mention anyone who engages in presumably less "dignified" practices such as polyamory and sex work.[10] It may also be bad news for the children of such persons, who seem likely to remain pawns in the nation's struggles over the prevailing definitions of family life.

As Wendy Brown's (1995) work predicts, the Court's willingness to protect the children of same-sex couples, and the couples themselves, was explicitly premised on the recognition of injuries to both groups.[11] To qualify for the Constitution's protections, both children and parents were legally required to identify themselves as vulnerable victims—literally "demeaned," "disrespected," "harmed," "humiliated," "injured," "stigmatized," and "wounded" (*Obergefell*: 2695–96) in the Court's terms. In *Windsor* and *Obergefell*, then, the balance of power swung from right to left, but the cult of the Child was reaffirmed (Edelman 2004: 19). Within the child protection paradigms presented by both parties, children were always at risk, in one way or another. The parties have now traded places in victory and defeat, but children have always been in need of protection—first from homosexuals, now from homophobes.

Of Nature and Nurture: *Obergefell*'s Gay Child

And what of the queer child now? After *Obergefell*, do we know where *our* children are?

Sadly, no. In *Obergefell*, the Court offers only one portrayal of children being raised by same-sex parents: the three adopted children of April DeBoer and Jayne Rowse. In the Court's account, the couple's children were always gendered, but they were never sexualized: "a baby boy," "another son," and "a baby girl" (2595). Despite the country's long-standing fears about the spread of homosexuality, the Court's opinions in *Windsor* and *Obergefell* offer no comment on the possibility of the protogay child—the elephant in the movement since long before Stonewall (Rosky 2013b: 618–64). In both opinions, the children of same-sex couples are explicitly recognized and protected, but the specter of a gay child remains invisible (Stockton 2009: 6–8).

Paradoxically, *Obergefell* does stake a claim that bears on the production of gay children—but for queers, it is the kind of claim that only makes matters worse. In a painful attempt to illustrate how the country's attitudes about homosexuality have evolved, the Court writes: "For much of the 20th century, . . . homosexuality was treated as an illness. . . . Only in more recent years have psychiatrists and others recognized that sexual orientation is both a normal expression of human sexuality and immutable" (2596).[12] Worse yet, the Court claims that the supposedly "immutable nature" of homosexuality is pertinent—and again, possibly prerequisite—to the success of the petitioner's constitutional claims. After insisting that the petitioners have come to praise marriage, not to bury it, the Court posits that same-sex couples have no other means to achieve such a sanctified status: "And their immutable nature dictates that same-sex marriage is their only real path to this profound commitment" (*Obergefell*: 2594).

The argument from immutability has many flaws, all of which have been amply documented by queer theorists and legal scholars, among many others.[13] Most fundamentally, the argument proceeds from the troubling premise that same-sex couples deserve civil rights only because "we can't help it" (Schmeiser 2009: 1520–21). In this sense, the immutability argument is an acquittal on an empirical technicality: a declaration that lesbian and gay people are innocent of homosexual choices, because, being "born that way," they had no meaningful alternatives to same-sex relationships. As one court explained: "Marrying a person of the opposite sex is an unrealistic option for gay and lesbian individuals (*Perry v. Schwarzenegger*: 969).

And it is not just gay adults who are innocent: it is the children of same-sex couples, too. In *Obergefell*, the Court stresses that children being raised by same-sex couples "suffer the significant material costs of being raised by unmarried parents, relegated *through no fault of their own* to a more difficult and uncertain family life" (2600). In short, we cannot punish the kids for the same reason that we cannot punish the parents. They are born into these families; they cannot help themselves. By claiming that homosexuality is "normal" and "immutable," the Court implies that homosexuality is natural. What a bummer! There is no one to blame.

By positing that homosexuality is "immutable," the Court implicitly presumes that gay adults were once gay children—or at least protogay children, or gay teenagers. Strangely, however, the Court says nothing more to specifically address the fear that allowing same-sex couples to marry could influence the sexual orientation of children—not only the children of same-sex couples but all "the children of America."[14] In this sense, the gay child is born in *Obergefell*, but it is kept just out of sight, and just out of mind. As Kathryn Bond Stockton (2009: 6–8) notes, the figure of the gay child exists only in the past, as an unmentioned memory in the childhood of gay adults. While the Court insists that the children of same-sex couples are wounded—"harmed" and "humiliated" (*Obergefell*: 2601)—it does not contemplate the possibility that gay and lesbian children are among them. Simply put, the sexuality of these children is not mentioned. In Stockton's (2009: 6) terms, the children of same-sex couples are asexual or desexualized—and yet they are implicitly presumed to be heterosexual.

The tragedy is that the battle over same-sex marriage did not have to end on such a sour note. Strictly speaking, the Court's claims about the dignity of marriage, the need to protect vulnerable kids, and the immutability of homosexuality were gratuitous. Without psychoanalyzing the justices' motives, one can say that the Court could easily have reached the same result without relying on such troubling premises. If anything, the claim of immutability stands in marked tension with the underlying logic of *Obergefell*: by upholding "the right to personal *choice* regarding marriage," the Court vindicated same-sex marriage as a matter of individual autonomy rather than equality among groups (2599; emphasis added). Quoting a 1967 ruling on interracial marriage, the Court observed: "The freedom to marry, or not marry . . . resides with the individual" (ibid., quoting *Loving v. Virginia*). If same-sex marriage is an option for everyone—a fundamental right—then it hardly matters whether anyone is "born" wanting to marry a person of the same sex.

While constitutional law is an imperfect vehicle for queer politics, the logic of the Supreme Court's earlier rulings—prior to *Windsor* and *Obergefell*—had left the Court ample room to adopt a more promising vision of the law's relationship to children's queerness. In the sections that follow, I give a brief genealogy—in queer theory, legal scholarship, and judicial opinions—of a constitutional claim for children's right to be queer.

The Early Years: Birthing the Gay Child

Since the earliest days of the LGBT movement, most advocates have responded to the opposition's fears of "recruiting" and "role modeling" by attempting to debunk them—to refute them with arguments based on empirical data (Rosky 2013b: 665–84). In one case after another, LGBT advocates have insisted that role modeling could not possibly work, because "the vast majority of lesbian and gay adults were raised by heterosexual parents" and "the vast majority of children raised by lesbian and gay parents eventually grow up to be heterosexual."[15] Above all, they have argued that children's sexual and gender development cannot be influenced by parents or teachers, because a person's sexual orientation and gender identity are fixed early in life and cannot be learned, taught, chosen, or changed.[16]

Yet even as early as Anita Bryant's campaign in the late 1970s, there were LGBT advocates who presented a more ambitious challenge to the opposition's recruiting and role modeling arguments. One notorious example was Bob Kunst, a Dade County activist whom Bryant had accused of handing out pamphlets about homosexuality at local high schools. Throughout Bryant's campaign, Kunst brazenly admitted that Dade County's antidiscrimination law would provide lesbian and gay youth with role models—indeed, he identified himself as "an absolutely positive role model" (Clendinen and Nagourney 1999: 301), and he claimed that providing children with gay role models was one of the antidiscrimination law's principal benefits (Fejes 2008: 81). In a public meeting at a local church in Miami, Kunst speculated that between 10 and 15 percent of children in Dade County were already "homosexual"—in his view, "people were inherently bisexual; an individual's specific sexuality was in many ways a matter of choice; the goal was to explore it" (ibid.: 131, 67). He was especially fond of drawing an analogy between sexuality and ice cream flavors: "Life is like ice-cream, there's 38 flavors out there, you choose the flavor you want" (ibid.: 68). He described his strategy in unapologetically radical terms, arguing that activists must "'expose the root of homophobic insecurity and call it like it is' and be 'outfront all the way through, redefining same-sex and both-sex experiences in terms of the beautiful new role models they represent'" (ibid.: 147). However naive Kunst may have seemed during this era, he was not alone in making such claims. In 1981 Gore Vidal wrote in the *Nation* that "a teacher known to be a same-sexer would be a splendid role model for those same-sexers that he—or she—is teaching" (512).

Queer theorists were not far behind. In 1989 Eve Kosofsky Sedgwick (1991: 18, 23) delivered a trail-blazing talk, "How to Bring Your Kids Up Gay: The War on Effeminate Boys," in which she railed against society's widespread "wish that gay people *not exist*" and, in particular, the lingering "desire for a nongay outcome" among childhood psychologists. In the early 1990s Sedgwick's battle cry was taken up by a new vanguard of scholars in other fields. In 1994, for example, the psychologist Laura Benkov observed that in custody and visitation cases involving a lesbian or gay parent, both sides tacitly assumed that children should be discouraged from becoming lesbian, gay, or bisexual. Although she acknowledged that "refuting the worry that children raised by homosexuals will themselves grow up to be gay was a pivotal step in the legal advocacy for homosexual parents," she emphasized that it was only the first step, because it sought to answer "homophobic questions on homophobic terms" (Benkov 1994: 62, 63). She lamented: "It seems society is not ready yet for a more deeply challenging response to the question of whether the kids of homosexuals will grow up to be gay—namely, *so what if they do?*" (ibid.: 63; emphasis added).

Meanwhile, legal and cultural theorists were moving quickly to develop Sedgwick's insights into the academy's first overtly legal and political arguments for the liberation of homosexuality, rather than the protection of homosexuals. In 1994 Janet Halley published a withering critique of the legal argument that gays should be protected by courts because sexual orientation is "immutable"; the following year, Lisa Duggan (1994: 8–9) urged queers to launch a "No Promo Hetero" campaign, in response to the opposition's rallying cry of "No Promo Homo." Although neither Halley nor Duggan focused specifically on the context of queerness in childhood, they both invoked Sedgwick's work to articulate universalizing claims on behalf of all queers—indeed, on behalf of all queerness—rather than the distinct minority of people who identify as lesbian, gay, or bisexual.

Minor Disregard: The Child's Right to Come Out

Within a few years, the law professor Teemu Ruskola (1996: 269) used the work of early queer theorists as a springboard from which to criticize "the legal construction of the fantasy that gay and lesbian youth do not exist." Even today, Ruskola's article "Minor Disregard" is still widely cited as the foundation of legal scholarship on homosexuality and childhood. In the wake of *Windsor* and *Obergefell*, his argument merits careful scrutiny as a kind of historical artifact of the modern LGBT movement: the legal academy's first brief for the judicial recognition of gay teens.

In this trailblazing article, Ruskola begins by explaining that according to "popular, medical, and legal understandings of homosexuality . . . gay kids are not gay but merely 'confused,'" and "there is no conceptual space for a coherently gay adolescent" (ibid.: 270). Above all, he locates this fantasy in "the seemingly indestructible myth of homosexual recruitment"—the axiom that homosexuals *must* recruit, because they cannot reproduce (ibid.: 273). After painting this grim portrait, Ruskola modestly argues that "gay kids deserve recognition, respect, and protection" (ibid.: 272). More than anything else, he emphasizes the *recognition* of gay youth—the act of naming children as "gay"—as the primary way to respect and protect them: "The first step in the protection of gay kids must be to *see* them as gay kids; unless the law is able to name the child, it will be unable to safeguard him or her" (ibid.: 273). Based on this principle, he sounds "a call for the law to recognize and protect the youth who identify themselves as gay and lesbian by *naming* them as gay and lesbian, rather than as confused, presumptively heterosexual future adults" (ibid.: 274; emphasis added).

In an especially provocative move, Ruskola means to challenge "the assumption that *kids* cannot be gay in the first place" by asking "what if homosexuality is not a matter of children's derailed sexual development, of kids *growing up* to be gay, but of *being* gay?" (ibid.: 319, 320). Against a world of doubt, he insists that children can be gay in the here and now, even before they are adults. He observes that despite the pervasive belief that homosexuality is only for adults, "it is a fact—and a miracle—that there are youth who, against all odds, self-identify as gay" (ibid.: 323). He emphasizes that "whether we call them gay kids or confused children matters a great deal," because "the act of renaming youth with same-sex erotic desires as gay or proto-gay has direct implications for what it means to protect them" (ibid.: 324).

It is no wonder that Ruskola's argument has been so influential and has stood up to the passage of time so well. Twenty years ago, it was both visionary and brave to offer such a full-throated defense of "gay and lesbian youth," when the sociology on this subject was still new (Ruskola 1996: 270n4) and queer theory had barely been discovered by law professors.[17] And despite Ruskola's (1996: 272, 274) polemical style, it is hard to quarrel with his basic principle that "gay kids deserve recognition, respect, and protection" or his modest proposal that "the law [should] recognize and protect the youth who identify themselves as gay and lesbian by naming them as gay and lesbian, rather than as confused." Yet Ruskola's argument seems to leave behind some of the normative challenges presented by those who preceded him—not only Kunst and Vidal, but Sedgwick and Benkov. Each of Ruskola's departures from this early work turns on his concept of gay and lesbian youth, which imposes three distinct limitations on the scope of his argument.

The first limitation is readily apparent: Ruskola leaves the "B" and the "T" out of "LGBT," along with the Q, I, and A, for that matter. Throughout the article, he uses advocates on behalf of "gay and lesbian youth." Although he invokes the phrase "queer kids" several times, he uses it synonymously with "gay and lesbian youth," rather than in any more inclusive manner. He makes only passing reference to bisexual children, and no reference to transgender, intersex, or asexual children at all. While these oversights are unfortunate, they are likely a product of the time in which Ruskola was writing. With the benefit of new insights, they are easy to fix. Rather than limit ourselves to a claim on behalf of "gay and lesbian youth," advocates can and do now insist that the law should recognize the sexuality and gender of all children, regardless of whether they happen to be lesbian, gay, bisexual, transgender, queer, intersex, or asexual.[18]

But Ruskola's use of the phrase "gay and lesbian youth" raises two other questions for queers—questions that are less obvious but more profound. The first is the mysterious way that Ruskola deploys the concept of youth, as if it were synonymous with the concept of child. Although he often insists that gay and lesbian youth *do* exist, he uses the term *youth* interchangeably with several others—*adolescent, teenager, minor, child,* and *kid*—which do not typically refer to the same stage in a person's development. In the opening paragraph, for example, he objects to the fantasy that "gay and lesbian *youth* do not exist," the belief that "gay *kids* are not gay but merely 'confused,'" and the lack of any "conceptual space for a coherently gay *adolescent*" (Ruskola 1996: 270; emphasis added). The problem is not that Ruskola leaves these terms undefined but that he conflates them in ways that confine homosexuality—reassuringly—to the teenage years. By using narrow terms like *adolescent* and *teenager* as substitutes for broader terms like *child* and *kid*, Ruskola seems to collapse the latter into the former—and thus to limit himself to a defense of homosexuality in adolescence. If we ultimately want to make room for a coherently gay *child*, then why object only that "there is no conceptual space for a coherently gay *adolescent?*" (ibid.: 270).[19]

This query raises the final limitation in Ruskola's argument: What *is* a "gay" or "lesbian" child—and what, for that matter, is a "bisexual" or "transgender" child? What precisely must a child think, say, or do to be considered "gay" or "lesbian" and thereby qualify for the law's protections? In this argument on behalf of "gay and lesbian youth," how is children's homosexuality defined—by reference to desire, behavior, relationship, identification, or by some combination of these criteria? To such questions, Ruskola gives a straightforward answer: he presumes that to qualify as "gay" or "lesbian" before the law, children must *identify* themselves in these terms. He emphasizes that "it is a fact—and a miracle—that there are youth who, against all odds, *self-identify* as gay," and he argues that "the law [should] recognize and protect the youth *who identify themselves* as gay and lesbian by naming them as gay and lesbian, rather than as confused" (ibid.: 323, 274; emphasis added).

This principle of self-identification is not problematic, as far as it goes: surely children should have the freedom to identify themselves as lesbian, gay, bisexual, or transgender, if they choose to. But as Sedgwick (1990: 42) once warned, "Many gay adults may never have been gay kids and some gay kids may not turn into gay adults," so the principle can and should be pushed a bit farther. What protections might the law offer to children who entertain same-sex fantasies, harbor same-sex desires, engage in same-sex behavior, and enter same-sex relationships—but are either unable or unwilling to identify as lesbian, gay, or even bisexual during childhood? What legal protections might exist for children who vary from traditional gender norms, but do not identify as transsexual or even transgender? Using queer theory as a guidepost, can lawyers and judges articulate claims not only for some children's right to identify as LGBTQIA, but for the potential of queerness in every child?

No Promo Hetero: Before the Law

It took several years before anything approaching Ruskola's vision was articulated by lawyers or adopted by courts. In two prominent cases—*Lawrence v. Texas* and *Perry v. Schwarzenegger*—lawyers and judges began to build a constitutional case for children's right to be queer. In *Lawrence v. Texas*, the attorney Paul Smith argued the case for John Lawrence and Tyron Garner, two men who had been convicted under a Texas sodomy law, before the United States Supreme Court.[20] In his opening argument, Smith told the justices that even when acts of sodomy were not criminally prosecuted, laws against sodomy were often invoked to justify discrimination against lesbian and gay people in other settings: "They're denied visitation to their own children, they're denied custody of children, they're denied public employment. They're denied private employment." In response, Chief Justice William Rehnquist asked Smith whether his argument could be used to challenge a school's preference for hiring heterosexual teachers: "If you prevail, Mr. Smith, and this law is struck down, do you think that would also mean that a State could not prefer heterosexuals to homosexuals to teach kindergarten?"

Smith had prepared for general questions about how legalizing sodomy would affect children's sexual development, but he had not anticipated this particular question about the constitutionality of discrimination against gay teachers (Carpenter 2012: 230). He cleared his throat, and for a moment, he seemed to grasp for a way to distinguish between the two policies. "I think the issue of—of preference in the educational context would involve very different criteria, Your Honor, and very different uh, uh—considerations." Regaining his footing, he proposed that "the State would have to come in with some sort of a justification."

Taking up Smith's challenge, Justice Antonin Scalia gamely asked whether the state's justification could be "the same that's alluded to here, disapproval of homosexuality." Smith replied, "Well, I think it would be highly—highly problematic, such a—justification . . . if that were the only justification that could be offered, there was not some showing that there would be any more concrete harm to the children in the school." Now that the tables had turned, it was Justice Scalia who seemed to struggle to express himself in suitable language: "Only that the children might—might—might be induced to, uh—to, to—to, to follow the path of homosexuality."

Given that Justice Scalia is rarely at a loss for words, the pauses in this sentence seem especially significant. In 1978, then-Justice Rehnquist had colorfully compared the contagiousness of homosexuality and measles;[21] by 2003, Justice Scalia was apparently uncomfortable speaking in such colorful metaphors. Rather than suggest that a gay teacher would "seduce," "indoctrinate," or "recruit" children into homosexuality, he felt compelled to articulate the fear of the queer child in more neutral terms. But in another sign of the times, Justice Scalia's attempt at subtlety did not seem to pay off with the spectators. As soon as he proffered the theory that "the child might be induced to follow the path of homosexuality," the noises from the gallery were audible: some laughed; others groaned.[22]

Of course, Smith did neither; he did not have such luxuries. He could have replied that Justice Scalia's claim was absurd because homosexuality was not a "path," or something that would "follow" from children being taught by gay teachers. But as Smith later explained, he did not want to get himself mired in "complicated questions of whether sexual orientation is genetic or developed, chosen or unchosen, fixed or immutable" (Carpenter 2012: 230). At the same time, however, he did not want to concede that Justice Scalia's claim was factually valid or that the state could legitimately prefer to hire heterosexuals as kindergarten teachers (ibid.). Instead of challenging Justice Scalia on empirical grounds, Smith replied that Justice Scalia's logic was essentially circular, because it was based on nothing more than disapproval of homosexual choices, or a preference for one group over another: "Well, I—I think the State has to have a greater justification for its discrimination than we prefer pushing people towards heterosexuality. That amounts to the same thing as disapproval of people's choices in this area and there has to be a more—more reasons and justifiable distinction than simply we prefer this group of people, the majority, instead of this group of people, the minority" (ibid.: 21). Without claiming that children were "born" gay—or more broadly, that homosexuality was "immutable"—Smith had revealed the state's concerns about children's heterosexual development as nothing more than a long-standing tradition of homophobia.

Seven years later, in the highly publicized case *Perry v. Schwarzenegger*, Chief Judge Vaughn Walker invalidated Proposition 8, the California ballot initiative that banned same-sex couples from marrying. In legal terms, Judge Walker's opinion was issued by a trial court, so it was not binding on courts outside California. But in cultural terms, it marked a significant step in the evolution of children's right to be queer. In his remarkable ruling, Judge Walker offered the judiciary's only explicit rejection of "the fear that exposing children to homosexuality will turn them into homosexuals" (1003).

During the ballot campaign for Prop 8, the law's sponsors had claimed that it would "protect our children from being taught in public schools that 'same-sex marriage' is the same as traditional marriage" (quoted in ibid.: 930). Because "state law may require teachers to instruct children as young as kindergarteners about marriage," they warned, "TEACHERS COULD BE REQUIRED to teach young children there is *no difference* between gay marriage and traditional marriage" (Prentice et al. 2008). To dramatize this danger, the campaign aired a television commercial in which a young girl tells her mother: "Mom, guess what I learned in school today? . . . I learned that a *prince* can marry a *prince*, and *I* can marry a *princess*!" (*Perry*: 990).

When Prop 8's sponsors were hauled into court, however, they took pains to distance themselves from the campaign's fiery rhetoric. Rather than claiming that Prop 8 could be justified by the notion that "exposure to homosexuality would turn children into homosexuals," they claimed that the law was designed only "to protect children from learning about same-sex marriage in school" (1003). Perhaps because they sensed the weakness of this argument, they declined to explain why children should be protected from learning about this particular subject. Instead, they sought to justify Prop 8 only on other grounds—as a way to preserve "the traditional institution of marriage," foster "naturally procreative relationships," and protect "the . . . rights of individuals and institutions that oppose same-sex marriage on religious and moral grounds" (998–1001).

Judge Walker was not fooled by this bait-and-switch tactic. Drawing on expert testimony to place the Prop 8 campaign in "historical context," the judge found that the campaign's advertisements "insinuated that learning about same-sex marriage could make a child gay or lesbian and that parents should dread having a gay or lesbian child" (998). Based on "the evidence at trial," he concluded that both of these fears were "completely unfounded" (1003).

At first glance, this sentence appears to be a classic restatement of the LGBT movement's immutability apologetics: "Don't worry folks, homosexuality is not contagious. Kids are born gay or straight, so there's nothing to fear." By invoking the facts, rather than the law, Judge Walker initially seems to attack the empirical premise that queerness *could* be contained, without challenging the normative premise that queerness *should* be contained. But a closer reading of *Perry* reveals that Judge Walker's reference to "the evidence presented at trial" is misleading, because it does not refer to the kind of evidence that one would expect—evidence that sexual orientation is immutable. Elsewhere in his ruling, Judge Walker offers a long list of "findings of fact"—eighty in all—based on his review of the evidence presented at trial (953–91). In one of these eighty findings, he does conclude that "individuals do not generally choose their sexual orientation" and that "no credible evidence supports a finding that an individual may, through conscious decision, therapeutic intervention or any other method, change his or her sexual orientation" (966). But he does not rely on this finding as one of the reasons for rejecting "the fear that exposing children to homosexuality would turn them into homosexuals" or the notion that "parents should dread having children who are not heterosexuals" (1003).

Instead, Judge Walker cites fourteen other findings to support his statement that "these fears were completely unfounded" (1003). His first finding is better characterized as a conclusion of law, rather than a finding of fact: "California has no interest in asking gays and lesbians to change their sexual orientation or in reducing the number of gays and lesbians in California" (967). Even if California could change gays and lesbians, he reasons, the government would not have any legitimate reason for doing so. Why not? Because, as he explained, "same-sex sexual orientation does not result in any impairment in judgment or general social and vocational capabilities," "sexual orientation is not related to an individual's ability to contribute to society or perform in the workplace," and finally, "same-sex couples are identical to opposite-sex couples in the characteristics relevant to the ability to form successful marital unions" (ibid.). Instead of finding that a person's sexual orientation is biologically determined, Walker declares that it just does not matter, because a person's sexual orientation is not legally relevant.

To assess how Judge Walker's argument builds on Ruskola's, it is helpful to compare the *Perry* opinion to Judge Robert Shelby's opinion in *Kitchen v. Herbert*, another highly publicized same-sex marriage case.[23] In 2013, shortly after *Windsor* was decided, Judge Shelby was asked to review the constitutionality of Amendment 3, Utah's law that banned same-sex couples from marrying (1181). As one would expect, Judge Shelby subjected Utah's law to the same framework that the Supreme Court had laid out in *Windsor*. After recognizing that "roughly 3,000 children are currently being raised by same-sex couples in Utah," Judge Shelby reasoned that "these children are . . . worthy of the State's protection, yet Amendment 3 harms them for the same reasons that the Supreme Court found that DOMA harmed the children of same-sex couples" (1212). Quoting extensively from *Windsor*, he explained that "Amendment 3 'humiliates . . . thousands of children now being raised by same-sex couples,'" and that "Amendment 3 'also brings financial harm to children of same-sex couples'" (ibid.). After laying out the Supreme Court's analysis of the harms in *Windsor*, Judge Shelby then extended the same principle to "children . . . who themselves are gay or lesbian" (1213): "Finally, Utah's prohibition of same-sex marriage further injures *the children of both opposite-sex and same-sex couples who themselves are gay or lesbian*, and who will grow up with the knowledge that the State does not believe they are as capable of creating a family as their heterosexual friends" (ibid.; emphasis added).

Responding to Ruskola's prophetic call, Judge Shelby pushed the law's recognition of gay children yet another step forward. Unlike the Supreme Court in *Obergefell*, Judge Shelby explicitly recognized that his jurisdiction included "children . . . who . . . *are* gay or lesbian," and he specifically imagined how the state's marriage laws would affect them. In this respect, Judge Shelby's opinion is even more ambitious than Judge Walker's: whereas Judge Walker imagined the *possibility* of a lesbian or gay child, Judge Shelby acknowledged the actual *existence* of "children who . . . are gay or lesbian."

Ultimately, however, Judge Shelby's analysis falls back on the gratuitous rhetoric of "harm" and "humiliation" articulated by the Supreme Court in *Windsor*. Rather than insisting that Utah had "no interest" in encouraging children to be heterosexual, he focused on how the state had injured "children who . . . are gay or lesbian." But as Paul Smith and Judge Walker demonstrate, the rhetorics of injury and identity are not only unfortunate but unrequired. To reject the fear of the queer child, lawyers and judges need not prove that sexual orientation is "immutable"—or even that some children really "are" lesbian, gay, or bisexual.

Drawing on a long line of Supreme Court cases before *Windsor* and *Obergefell*, they can maintain that the state has no interest in promoting heteronormativity during childhood, for the same reasons that it has no interest in promoting heteronormativity at any age. Simply put, the state can offer no independent justification for encouraging children to be "straight" or discouraging them from being "queer." As a result, the state must adopt a neutral stance vis-à-vis the trajectory of children's sexual and gender development. Borrowing from Duggan's "Queering the State" (1994), we might call this the doctrine of "No Promo Hetero."

I have published an extended analysis of the constitutional foundations for this claim in other work (Rosky 2013a: 434–500), so I sketch only the broad contours of my legal argument here. Building on a schema familiar to legal scholarship on LGBT rights, No Promo Hetero challenges the state's interest in promoting heterosexuality in childhood by articulating a tripartite defense of children's speech, status, and conduct. It argues that these three aspects of children's sexuality and gender are connected to and protected by the Constitution's free speech, equal protection, and due process guarantees. When the state asserts that the promotion of heteronormativity in childhood is a legitimate state interest, it violates at least one if not all of these guarantees. When the state targets children's speech, it engages in a form of "viewpoint discrimination" that violates the free speech protections of the First and Fourteenth Amendments (ibid.: 436–44, 465–69). When the state targets children's status, it betrays a form of "class-based animus" that violates the equal protection guarantees of the Fifth and Fourteenth Amendments (ibid.: 444–53, 469–73). When the state targets children's relationships, it evinces a form of "moral disapproval" that violates the due process protections of the Fifth and Fourteenth Amendments (ibid.: 453–58, 473–78). Taken together, these constitutional guarantees prohibit the state from attempting to regulate the sexual and gender valence of children's speech, status, and conduct. By doing so, they establish every child's right to be queer.

The latter claim may seem surprising, given that the arguments presented by Smith and Walker were focused exclusively on the state's authority to prevent *adults* from influencing children's sexual and gender development. But a child's right to be queer follows logically from traditional liberal understandings of the relationship between the state's authority and individual rights. In the legal imaginary of the United States, individual liberty has traditionally been conceptualized in negative terms—as a freedom *from* governmental restraints, rather than an entitlement *to* governmental benefits.[24] Within this syllogism, every limit on the government's authority can be understood as an individual right and vice versa.

In light of this logic, the doctrine of No Promo Hetero inherently entails every child's right to be queer. Like all children's rights—indeed, like all constitutional rights—a child's right to be queer is not absolute. It must be balanced against a parent's right to direct the care, custody, and control of her child and the state's interest in protecting all children's welfare. But within these parameters, every child has a right to an "open future" in sexual and gender development—at the very least, an equal liberty to be straight or queer.[25]

Law's Limits

Of course, even if this claim of No Promo Hetero were vindicated by the Supreme Court, it too would offer no panacea for queers. As Duggan (1994: 10–11) herself cautions, "Because this case is formulated within the terms of liberalism, it may trap us in as many ways as it releases us." In particular, Duggan worries that No Promo Hetero "seems to construct a zone of liberty in negative relation to the state," insofar as "it argues about what the state canNOT do" (ibid.: 11).[26] Duggan's qualms about the limits of liberalism are especially relevant in the context of childhood. Because children are less physically and emotionally developed than adults, they do not enjoy the same degree of autonomy, especially with regard to sexuality and gender.

At the most obvious level, the Constitution does not grant children the legal authority to consent to sexual relations. Although the age of sexual consent varies from state to state, it falls between the ages of sixteen and eighteen in all US jurisdictions. In the 1970s, when a plaintiff asked the Supreme Court to recognize "a right of minors as well as adults to engage in private consensual sexual behavior," two justices wrote separately to reject this claim as "frivolous."[27] Even in *Lawrence v. Texas*—which recognized the individual's liberty to choose homosexual relationships—the Court emphasized that "the present case does not involve minors" but rather "two adults who, with full and mutual consent from each other, engaged in sexual practices common to a homosexual lifestyle."[28]

In addition, the regulation of children's sexual and gender development is substantially privatized: it is governed by family, friends, surrogates, and social norms more than teachers, judges, and legal rules. And within the domain of family law, it is parents who rule the roost. Nearly one hundred years ago, the Supreme Court held that parents have the fundamental right to direct the care, custody, and control of a child,[29] and the Court has reaffirmed this principle in recent years.[30] Under this doctrine, the state must presume that a parent acts in her child's best interests unless a court determines that the child has been abused or neglected, or that the parent is no longer fit to care for the child.[31]

Whatever one thinks of these distributions of power among parent, state, and child, the doctrine of No Promo Hetero need not disrupt them. Within broad boundaries, the principle allows the government to prohibit children from engaging in sexual relations, just as the laws in all fifty states already do. This does not imply, however, that the principle has no bearing on children's sexual liberties. In *State v. Limon*, for example, the Kansas Supreme Court struck down a law that imposed harsher punishments on minors who engaged in same-sex behavior than minors who engaged in other-sex behavior.[32] Similarly, in *Nguon v. Wolf*, a federal court in California held that a public school could not discipline students for displaying same-sex affections unless it imposed the same sanctions on students for displaying other-sex affections.[33] And finally, in *McMillen v. Itawamba County School District*, a federal court in Mississippi ruled that a public school could not prohibit a female student from bringing her girlfriend to the prom or wearing a tuxedo.[34] Even if the Constitution does not offer children a broad liberty to engage in sexual conduct, it still protects every child's *equal* liberty to choose between same-sex or other-sex conduct.[35]

Within similarly broad boundaries, the principle of No Promo Hetero permits parents to do precisely what it prohibits the government from doing— attempting to influence the trajectory of children's sexual and gender development. Under this regime, some parents would encourage children to be straight, others would encourage them to be queer, and still others would take a neutral stance, granting children the freedom to answer such questions for themselves. But within what boundaries? For present purposes, the existing body of abuse and neglect law provides a plausible starting point. At a minimum, federal law effectively establishes that parents may not act in a manner that causes a child's "death, serious physical or emotional harm, sexual abuse, or exploitation, or . . . presents an imminent risk of serious harm."[36] So even if parents attempt to encourage children to be straight or discourage children from being queer, they may not do so in any manner that poses an imminent risk of serious harm.

Like many child welfare determinations, such cases would turn on the prevailing consensus of physicians, psychiatrists, and psychologists who study child development. During the past several decades, a broad consensus has developed among medical professionals that homosexuality is not a mental illness and that therapies aimed at changing a minor's sexual orientation are harmful and dangerous (American Academy of Pediatrics et al. 2008). By contrast, the American Psychiatric Association has only recently taken steps to destigmatize the diagnosis of "Gender Identity Disorder," which is now known as "Gender Dysphoria" (American Psychiatric Association 2013: 512). Even now, some licensed physicians continue to support "corrective therapy" for children who receive this diagnosis.[37] Unless and until a new consensus emerges, courts may be less willing to conclude that forcing a child into corrective therapy for "Gender Identity Disorder of Childhood" is a form of abuse or neglect.[38]

But if we focus only on traditional settings in which the state stands in the background—a husband and wife raising a child together—we miss the most powerful thrust of No Promo Hetero. Liberal mythology aside, the state acts in loco parentis in a long list of ways, intervening both directly and indirectly in children's sexual and gender development. Adoption and foster care are only the most obvious examples. When parents litigate custody and visitation disputes, they are subject to judicial determinations of children's best interests.[39] In public schools, the modern state is ubiquitous—in the hiring and firing of teachers, the setting of curriculums, even the acquisition of library books.[40] In public hospitals, physicians routinely designate newborns as "male" or "female" and prescribe cosmetic genital surgeries and hormone treatments for children who fall outside the binary model of gender and sex.[41] Under the regime of No Promo Hetero, the fear of the queer child would be banished from all these settings.

In *Obergefell*, the Supreme Court reassured the nation that the children of same-sex couples—and the couples themselves—would dignify marriage and be dignified by it. In this historic moment, the Court implied that society's long-standing concerns about the spread of homosexuality were misplaced, because "sexual orientation is both a normal expression of human sexuality and immutable" (2596).

Forty years after the rise of the modern LGBT movement, the time has come to defend children's queerness on its own terms, rather than assuring the world that homosexuality and gender variance can be quarantined. The state does not have any legitimate interest in promoting heteronormativity in childhood, for the same reasons that it does not have any interest in promoting heteronormativity at any age. The Constitution protects every child's right to an open future in sexual and gender development—an equal liberty to be straight or queer.

Notes

I am grateful to the University of Chicago, the University of Indiana–Bloomington, the University of Utah, and the Association of Law, Culture and the Humanities for the opportunity to present early drafts of this article. I would like to thank Carlos Ball, Michael Boucai, Emily Buss, Mary Anne Case, Anne Dailey, Julian Gill-Peterson, Michael Grossberg, Elizabeth Freeman, Rebekah Sheldon, and Kathryn Bond Stockton, as well as two peer reviewers, for providing thoughtful feedback.

1. *United States v. Windsor*, 133 S. Ct. 2675, 2013. Hereafter cited by page number.
2. *Obergefell v. Hodges*, 135 S. Ct. 2584, 2015. Hereafter cited by page number.
3. Cf. Stuart Hall et al. (1978: 220) defining "the signification spiral" as "a self-amplifying sequence within the area of signification: the activity or event with which the signification deals is escalated—made to seem more threatening—within the course of signification itself."
4. See *Black's Law Dictionary*, 6th ed., s.v. "obiter dictum": "an observation or remark made by a judge in pronouncing an opinion . . . [that is] not necessarily involved in the case or essential to its determination."
5. *Perry v. Schwarzenegger*, 704 F. Supp. 2d 921, 1003 (N.D. Cal. 2010). Hereafter cited by page number.
6. Brief on the Merits for Respondent the Bipartisan Legal Advisory Group of the U.S. House of Representatives at 48, *United States v. Windsor*, 133 S. Ct. 2675 (2013) (No. 12-307).
7. 142 Cong. Rec. H7491 (daily ed. July 12, 1996) (statement of Rep. Canady).
8. 142 Cong. Rec. H7491 (daily ed. July 12, 1996) (statement of Rep. Canady).
9. H.R. Rep. No. 104-664, at 15 n.53 (1996), reprinted in 1996 U.S.C.C.A.N. 2905, 2919 n.53.
10. Franke (2004: 1399, 1413): "The subjects of gay and lesbian political organizing at this moment have become same-sex couples, not persons who seek nonnormative kinship formations or individuals who engage in nonnormative sex"; Butler (2002: 229, 230–31), calling on queers to "attend to the foreclosure of the possible that takes place when, from the urgency to stake a political claim, one naturalizes the options that figure most legibly within the sexual field"; and Berlant (1998: 281, 286): "Why, when there are so many people, only one plot counts as 'life' (first comes love, then . . .)? Those who don't or can't find their way into that story—the queers, the single, the something else—can become so easily unimaginable, even often to themselves."
11. Brown (1995: 134): "Historically, rights have been claimed to secure formal emancipation for individuals stigmatized, traumatized, and subordinated by particular social identities, to secure a place for such individuals in a humanist discourse of universal personhood. . . . when they are 'brought into discourse,' rights are more likely to become sites of the production and regulation of identity as injury than vehicles of emancipation."
12. The Court does not say precisely what it means by the term *immutable*, but it hardly matters. In an earlier case, the Court claimed "sex" was "an immutable characteristic" because it was "determined solely by the accident of birth" and therefore did not bear any "relationship to individual responsibility" (*Frontiero v. Richardson*, 411 U.S. 677, 686 (1973) (plurality)).
13. See, e.g., Clarke 2015; Schmeiser 2009: 1520–21; Boucai 2012: 415, 168; Warner 1999: 9; Balkin 1997; Halley 1994: 503; and Sedgwick 1990: 41–44.

14. 142 Cong. Rec. H7491 (daily ed. July 12, 1996).

15. See, e.g., American Psychological Association 2006: 22–23. This claim has been included in numerous amicus briefs filed in support of challenges to laws prohibiting same-sex marriage and adoption by same-sex couples, and it has long been a staple of legal scholarship on lesbian and gay parenting. See Rosky 2013a: 429n12.

16. See, e.g., Brief for Appellees, *Perry v. Brown*, 671 F.3d 1052 (9th Cir. 2010) (No. 10-16696), 63: "The vast majority of gays and lesbians have little or no choice in their sexual orientation; and therapeutic efforts to change an individual's sexual orientation have not been shown to be effective and instead pose a risk of harm to the individual."

17. In 1995 Valdes called for "the initiation of Queer legal scholarship as a theoretical and political enterprise" (334).

18. The reasons for doing so are manifold. Most obviously, bisexual, transgender, queer, intersex, and asexual children exist, and they suffer from many of the same harms that lesbian and gay children do. They, too, should be protected from these harms, for the simple reason that all people should. More subtly, however, any specific attempt to protect lesbian and gay children—i.e., to establish protections that include only lesbian and gay children, without parallel protections for BTQIA children—is likely to be self-defeating. Of course, the distinctions among LGBTQIA children are conceptually important, and they correspond to meaningful differences in children's lives. But in light of the long tradition of conflating children's homosexuality, bisexuality, and gender variance in anti-LGBT discourse, it is vital that legal protections are designed broadly to include all these concepts. To take just a few examples: for decades, medical and legal authorities have claimed that children pass through a phase of "bisexuality" as they develop toward heterosexual adulthood—a phase that is used to justify shielding children from exposure to gay and bisexual adults, and to refute children's attempts to come out as gay or bisexual. Similarly, boys use "sissy" and "fag" interchangeably on the playground, and opponents often claim that children who come out as gay or transgender are both "confused." Given the opposition's tendency to conflate children's queerness along multiple axes, the fear of the queer child should be answered with legal protections that present a unified front. Advocates should defend BTQIA children to the same extent—and when possible, in the same breath—that they defend lesbian and gay children. As Sedgwick (1991: 20) writes, "To begin to theorize gender and sexuality as distinct though intimately entangled axes of analysis has been, indeed, a great advance of recent lesbian and gay thought. There is a danger, however, that that advance may leave the effeminate boy once more in the position of the haunting abject—this time the haunting abject of gay thought itself."

19. Of course, Ruskola likely had pragmatic reasons for limiting himself to a defense of gay adolescence: in 1996 it was radical enough to ask judges to recognize, respect, and protect gay teens, without calling to mind the existence of gay toddlers. And Ruskola surely knew that once courts established a bulwark for the equal protection of gay

teens, advocates would someday invoke this principle on behalf of gay children at any age. Indeed, this kind of incrementalism has long been evident in advocacy on behalf of children's queerness. As early as the 1970s, gay liberation groups were organizing on college campuses, but it was not until the 1990s that the Gay, Lesbian & Straight Education Network took on the issue of gay-straight alliances in secondary schools, and it was not until 2012 that GLSEN broached the touchy subject of "homophobia, gender expression and LGBT-inclusive family diversity at the elementary school level" (GLSEN and Harris Interactive 2012: title page). Yet however useful such stalling tactics may have been in 1996, they are beginning to seem dated now. As Kathryn Bond Stockton (2009: 6–7) observes, our popular and academic discourses have finally begun to admit the possibility of gay "youths" and "gay teenagers," and we have even begun to speak of gay "children" in the past tense—such as when Oprah Winfrey says of a guest on her talk show, "he knew he was gay at age four." Yet even now, both our courts and our culture remain hesitant to recognize that a "child" can be "gay" or "lesbian" in the present tense.

20. Transcript of oral argument in *Lawrence v. Texas*, 539 US 558, No. 02-102. The quotations that follow are based on the audio recording, which is available at www.oyez .org/cases/2002/02-102.

21. *Ratchford v. Gay Lib*, 434 U.S. 1080, 1084 (1978), Rehnquist, J., dissenting.

22. Compare Yoshino 2006: 206 with Carpenter 2012: 231.

23. *Kitchen v. Herbert*, 961 F.Supp.2d 1181 (D. Utah Dec. 20, 2013). Hereafter cited in the text.

24. In his dissent from *Obergefell*, Justice Clarence Thomas claimed that the majority's understanding of the "freedom to marry" represented a troubling exception to this general rule (2634). See also Franke 2004: 1414 ("It is wrong to understand the fight for gay marriage as a fight for sexual freedom or, for that matter, relationship-based freedom. Marriage is not a freedom. Rather, it is a *power*").

25. See Feinberg 1980, 124; and Rachmilovitz 2014: 1374.

26. To guard against this risk, Duggan (1994: 11) recommends "carefully fram[ing]" the argument, first, "to emphasize that state institutions must be evenhanded in the arena of sexuality, not that sexuality should be removed from state action completely," and second, to "make the crucial distinction between state institutions (which must, in some sense, be neutral) and 'the public' arena, where explicit advocacy is not only allowable but desirable."

27. *Carey v. Population Services International*, 431 U.S. 678, 702–703 (1977).

28. *Lawrence v. Texas*, 539 U.S. 558, 578 (2003).

29. *Meyer v. Nebraska*, 262 U.S. 390 (1923); *Pierce v. Society of Sisters*, 268 U.S. 510 (1925).

30. *Troxel v. Granville*, 530 U.S. 57, 65 (2000).

31. *Stanley v. Illinois*, 405 U.S. 645, 658 (1972).

32. *State v. Limon*, 122 P.3d 22 (Kan. 2005).

33. *Nguon v. Wolf*, 517 F. Supp. 2d at 1177 (C.D. Cal. 2007).

34. *McMillen v. Itawamba County School District*, 702 F. Supp. 2d 699 (N.D. Miss. 2010).

35. Although No Promo Hetero does not challenge the law's sweeping prohibitions against children's sexual behavior, it does not thereby reintroduce the narrative of the "innocent child" by way of the vulnerable gay child. To be sure, this "innocence narrative" is available, and it is increasingly commonplace in discussions of the gay child. See, e.g., *Gillman v. School Board for Holmes County*, 567 F. Supp. 2d 1359, 1370 (N.D. Fla. 2008) (arguing that a principal's targeting of gay and lesbian students "is particularly deplorable in light of studies which confirm the vulnerability of gay and lesbian students"); and Gilden (2013: 357) (tracking the use of a "gay teen innocence narrative" in several legal and cultural contexts). But in contrast to Ruskola's defense of "gay and lesbian youth," the principle of No Promo Hetero does not depend on identifying any children as LGBT or even identifying anyone as a "child." On the contrary, No Promo Hetero claims that these questions of identity are irrelevant, because the government has no interest in promoting heteronormativity at any age.

36. Child Abuse Prevention and Treatment Act Reauthorization Act of 2010, Pub. L. No. 111-320, § 142, 124 Stat. 3482.

37. Erika Skougard (2011: 1161, 1162–63) observes that "childhood gender experts are sharply divided about the best treatment for . . . children" who are diagnosed with "Gender Identity Disorder of Childhood."

38. See Skougard 2011. In recent years, some legislatures have attempted to resolve this issue on a statewide level by adopting a law that prohibits the practice of "conversion therapy" on minors, effectively establishing that this practice is a form of child abuse. See Eckholm 2012. Although these laws prohibit "sexual orientation change efforts," they define this term to include "efforts to change behaviors or *gender expressions*," as well as efforts "to eliminate or reduce sexual or romantic attractions or feelings toward individuals of the same sex" (California Business and Professions Code § 865(b)(1) (West 2013); emphasis added).

39. Rosky (2009: 257, 294–98) observes that in custody and visitation cases, litigants, experts, and judges often express concerns that lesbian and gay parents will serve as "role models," influencing children's sexual and gender development.

40. On teachers, see *Gaylord v. Tacoma Sch. Dist. No. 10*, 559 1340, 1347 P.2d (Wash. 1977), upholding the firing of a gay teacher based on "danger of encouraging expression of approval and of imitation" because "such students could treat the retention of the high school teacher by the school board as indicating adult approval of his homosexuality." On curricula, see *Parker v. Hurley*, 514 F.3d 87 (1st Cir. 2008), affirming dismissal of claims by parents seeking to exempt children from "indoctrination" through elementary school lessons featuring children's books about same-sex couples. On libraries, see *Board of Education v. Pico*, 457 U.S. 853 (1982), invalidating a

school board's decision to remove "filthy" books from libraries at high schools and junior high schools.

41. See Greenberg 2012: 11–26.

References

American Academy of Pediatrics et al. 2008. *Just the Facts about Sexual Orientation and Youth: A Primer for Principals, Educators, and School Personnel.* www.apa.org /pi/lgbt/resources/just-the-facts.pdf.

American Psychiatric Association. 2013. *Diagnostic and Statistical Manual of Mental Disorders.* 5th ed. Arlington, VA: American Psychiatric Association.

American Psychological Association. 2006. Brief of Amicus Curiae in Support of Plaintiffs-Appellees for Citizens for *Equal Prot. v. Bruning.* 455 F.3d 859 (8th Cir.) (No. 05-2604).

Balkin, Jack. 1997. "The Constitution of Status." *Yale Law Journal*, no. 106: 2313–74.

Benkov, Laura. 1994. *Reinventing the Family: The Emerging Story of Lesbian and Gay Parents.* New York: Crown.

Berlant, Lauren. 1997. *The Queen of America Goes to Washington City: Essays on Sex and Citizenship.* Durham, NC: Duke University Press.

———. 1998. "Intimacy: A Special Issue." *Critical Inquiry*, no. 24.

Boucai, Michael. 2012. "Sexual Liberty and Same-Sex Marriage: The Argument from Bisexuality." *San Diego Law Review* 49, no. 2: 168, 415–53.

Brown, Wendy. 1995. *States of Injury: Power and Freedom in Late Modernity.* Princeton: Princeton University Press.

Butler, Judith. 2002. "Is Kinship Always Already Heterosexual?" In *Left Legalism / Left Critique*, edited by Wendy Brown and Janet Halley, 229–58. Durham, NC: Duke University Press.

Carpenter, Dale. 2012. *Flagrant Conduct: The Story of Lawrence v. Texas: How a Bedroom Arrest Decriminalized Gay Americans.* New York: Norton.

Clarke, Jessica. 2015. "Against Immutability." *Yale Law Journal* 125, no. 1. www .yalelawjournal.org/article/against-immutability.

Clendinen, Dudley, and Adam Nagourney. 1999. *Out for Good: The Struggle to Build a Gay Rights Movement in America.* New York: Simon and Schuster.

Duggan, Lisa. 1994. "Queering the State." *Social Text*, no. 39: 1–14.

Eckholm, Erik. 2012. "Gay 'Cure' for Minors Is Banned in California." *New York Times*, October 1.

Edelman, Lee. 2004. *No Future: Queer Theory and the Death Drive.* Durham, NC: Duke University Press.

Feinberg, Joel. 1980. "The Child's Right to an Open Future." In *Whose Child? Children's*

Rights, Parental Authority, and State Power, edited by William Aiken and Hugh LaFollette, 124–53. Totowa, NJ: Rowman and Littlefield.

Fejes, Fred. 2008. *Gay Rights and Moral Panic: The Origins of America's Debate on Homosexuality*. New York: Palgrave Macmillan.

Franke, Katherine. 2004. "The Domesticated Liberty of *Lawrence v. Texas*." *Columbia Law Review* 104: 1399–1527.

Gilden, Andrew. 2013. "Cyberbullying and the Innocence Narrative." *Harvard Civil Rights–Civil Liberties Law Review* 48: 357–407.

Greenberg, Julie A. 2012. *Intersexuality and the Law: Why Sex Matters*. New York: New York University Press.

GLSEN and Harris Interactive. 2012. *Playgrounds and Prejudice: Elementary School Climate in the United States, A Survey of Students and Teachers*. New York: GLSEN.

Hall, Stuart, et al. 1978. *Policing the Crisis: Mugging, the State, and Law and Order*. New York: Palgrave Macmillan.

Halley, Janet. 1994. "Sexual Orientation and the Politics of Biology: A Critique of the Argument from Immutability." *Stanford Law Review* 36, no. 3: 503–68.

Prentice, Ron, et al. 2008. *Arguments in Favor of Proposition 8*. California General Election Official Voter Information Guide. vigarchive.sos.ca.gov/2008/general/argu-rebut/argu-rebutt8.htm.

Rachmilovitz, Orly. 2014. "Family Assimilation Demands and Sexual Minority Youth." *Minnesota Law Review*, no. 98: 1374–1452.

Rosky, Clifford J. 2009. "Like Father, Like Son: Homosexuality, Parenthood, and the Gender of Homophobia." *Yale Journal of Law and Feminism* 20, no. 2: 257–355.

———. 2013a. "No Promo Hetero: Children's Right to Be Queer." *Cardozo Law Review* 35: 425–510.

———. 2013b. "Fear of the Queer Child." *Buffalo Law Review*, no. 61: 607–97.

Ruskola, Teemu. 1996. "Minor Disregard: The Legal Construction of the Fantasy That Gay and Lesbian Youth Do Not Exist." *Yale Journal of Law and Feminism* 8, no. 2: 269–331.

Schmeiser, Susan R. 2009. "Changing the Immutable." *Connecticut Law Review* 41, no. 5: 1495–1522.

Sedgwick, Eve Kosofsky. 1990. *Epistemology of the Closet*. Berkeley: University of California Press.

———. 1991. "How to Bring Your Kids Up Gay." *Social Text*, no. 29: 18–27.

Skougard, Erika D. 2011. "The Best Interests of Transgender Children." *Utah Law Review*, no. 3: 1161–1201.

Stockton, Kathryn Bond. 2009. *The Queer Child, or Growing Sideways in the Twentieth Century*. Durham, NC: Duke University Press.

Valdes, Francisco. 1995. "Queer Legal Theory." *California Law Review* 83, no. 1: 344–77.

Vidal, Gore. 1981. "Some Jews and the Gays." *Nation*, November 14, 508–17.

Warner, Michael. 1999. *The Trouble with Normal: Sex, Politics, and the Ethics of Queer Life*. Cambridge, MA: Harvard University Press.

Yoshino, Kenji. 2006. *Covering: The Hidden Assault on Our Civil Rights*. New York: Random House.

THE STREET, THE SPONGE, AND THE ULTRA

Queer Logics of Children's Rebellion and Political Infantilization

Paul Amar

$\mathcal{A}$ confluence of global political maelstroms around the assertions and movement of very young people would seem to demand that scholars and activists grapple much more seriously with the "childness" of these collective actions and the forms of agency that generate them. In 2014, for instance, "surges" of preadolescents from El Salvador and Honduras—many between six and nine years old—confronted immigration enforcement officers at the US southern border (Park 2014).[1] In the Middle East, children continued to take to the streets on their own terms: preteen protesters flooded the streets of Palestine and Yemen by the thousands, hurling their bodies against police barriers and security perimeters (Frykberg 2015). In Brazil prepubescent black *favelado* residents launched the "rolezinho" movement, challenging the forces of militarization, exclusivism, and eviction around World Cup and Olympic developments by strolling, dragging themselves in carefree ways, and dancing en masse through elite shopping malls and gated communities (Pinho 2014) not as a march but as a repacing, taking a different pace and stepping of the collective body—demonstrations that were countered by explosive levels of police brutality, even lynching and mutilation. Even the most mainstream of infantilizing humanitarian agencies seemed to begin to recognize and honor children's agency in this tumultuous period. In 2014, at age sixteen, Malala Yousefzai was awarded the Nobel Peace Prize for her activism around girls' rights to education in Pakistan. She began her activist work at age ten. When Malala was twelve, the Taliban targeted her in an operation that merged tactics of child extermination, gendered war crime, and political assassination.

GLQ 22:4
DOI 10.1215/10642684-3603102
© 2016 by Duke University Press

In this study, I zero in on a particularly dynamic node of erupting and shifting childness. I examine the case of contemporary Egypt. I argue that in this country scholar-activists and structural antagonisms between children-driven movements and child-targeting regimes are generating new sets of global theories and traveling concepts. They are revealing the workings of political movements in which groups of children acting sometimes without adult guidance or supervision challenge global barriers of exclusion in polities like Egypt that are riven with popular contention and police reaction. In this context, I argue that the category of the child has come to signify a sexually polymorphous perversity as well as a politically insurgent potentiality. In this work I build on the illuminating findings of Omnia El Shakry (2011: 591) on how Egyptian nationalists configured the category of "youth" as an "insurgent subject" in the early twentieth century while shaping the child as an object of "structured, scientific play" under tutelage of reeducated motherhood (El Shakry 1998: 126; 2007: 132–35). I also draw on Rania Kassab Sweis's (2012: 47–48) pioneering analysis of contemporary non-governmental organization (NGO) elaborations of "transnational regimes of care" through experiments in protecting and politicizing care for adolescent girls in the villages of Egypt. And I build on Iman Bibars's (1998: 201) interview-based field-work with "at-risk" children and her early tracking of the emergence of punitive moral and legislative regimes around "street children" in Egypt and in the trans-national context in the 1990s. Although my new findings here seem to demonstrate that in the contemporary period the figure of "child" and "play" has moved from the realm of pedagogy and NGO care toward securitization and confrontation, the figure of the child has come to occupy the space of radical insurgent subjectivity, displacing to some extent "youth," their older postadolescent siblings. I am also building on the research of Sara Pursely (2013: 189), who, in examining mid-twentieth-century Iraq, suggests that "Middle Eastern discourses and experiences of 'youth' in this period could not have been merely an adoption or re-enactment of European and American discourses and experiences, for the simple reason that they were differently located within the universal spatiotemporal recapitulation narratives aligning national, racial, and individual-psychological development." Following these research leads, the present article demonstrates how children are besieged by subtly evolving security regimes deployed by repressive state apparatuses, especially the post-2011 revanchist "human security state" (Amar 2013: 1–38). Children in turn confront the infantilizing humanitarian logics of campaigns against child labor and human trafficking. These campaigns are infused with paternalism and moralism that condition liberals to see *horror*—not agency or history or politics—when confronted with the labor practices, mobility circuits, and sexual expressions that constitute the material and social conditions of young lives. When faced with the same phenomena, neo-authoritarians see *terror*, perceiving out-of-place infancy and children's collectives as menacing public order and state sovereignty in the form of thug groups, junior hooligan squads, or quasi-military threats.

Metaphors of infantilization seem repugnant when their racial or historical resonances are highlighted. Progressives reject the racialized infantilization of workers in colonial and neocolonial labor regimes—the lifelong "boy" appellation of black men in Jim Crow America (Bernstein 2011: 16), or the creepy quasi daughter status of adult domestic laborers in today's Persian Gulf or Brazil. We mobilize to stop the infantilization of women by global anti-abortion or anti–sex trafficking campaigns that attack bodily autonomy or that aim to detain, remother, and morally reeducate women. We critique twenty-first-century forms of humanitarian warfare that build legitimacy through infantilizing others, suppressing questions of civil, social, and economic engagement while rendering victim populations as mute, generic "womenandchildren" (Enloe 1990; Mikdashi 2014), naturalizing self-serving paternalism and a bombers'-eye view of "the responsibility to protect." These critiques have so powerfully interrogated how gender/race/colonial/indigenous subjects, as adults, are infantilized. But, oddly, these critiques have tended to avoid confronting the agency of the quintessential subject of infantilization itself, the child.

With all these critiques, it would seem "the infantilized" can only be a pernicious category designed to control various populations. So to take the next step, one may ask: Beyond these control functionalities does the child exist? Can the child persist as an unproblematic or natural category of the (sub)human after global machinations of infantilization have been revealed as fundamentally dehumanizing? By what political expediencies do children remain ruled not as agents but as spectacles of compelling innocence, securitizing horror, and developmentalist dependency?

As I demonstrate, collectives of children have responded in meaningful, patterned ways that resist or even threaten to overthrow these modes of infantilization and repression. Their actions are often strongly repressed by the state, but they also tend to be written off by analysts. The label of "street" evokes a polymorphous violation of class, community, circulation, and sexual norms that represent children as specters of pure chaos rather than as vehicles for collective human claims or as agents of socially self-organized resistance. As I explore here, recent revivals of the "problematic of street kids," whether deployed by the police state or humanitarian NGO, in global discourse or by the Egyptian state, reestablish the notion of the natural and normative (and thus infantile) child as they target its hyperexposed, publicly mobile opposite. This binary between kid-in-street and child-in-home blocks more nuanced legibilities.

Through the political processes that I enumerate below, children are governmentalized as "the last savages." The category or field of children is figured as a protection camp containing the last wholly wild human subjects whose "natural" or quintessential infantility, indiscipline, excess, and perversity remain largely uncontested, even by the critiques and resistances articulated by movements against racism, misogyny, indigenous dispossession, and coloniality. Patricia Crain (1999: 545) describes childhood or childness as "the last refuge of unexamined essentialism," and Cindy Katz (2008: 8), in "Childhood as Spectacle," states that "when it comes to children, we seem able to see them as innocent, unformed, as savage, as 'good' or as vulnerable without historicizing, locating, or specifying their much more complicated unstable and contingent subjectivity." Taking up the challenge to historicize, locate, and ground the subjectivity of "children," this article demonstrates how the exceptionalism of the "child as last savage" undergirds a transformed and intensified security regime and, very importantly, generates fertile conditions for explosive forms of mobilization by "children" themselves, whose actions tend to remain illegible to erstwhile political allies as well as opaque for most scholarly research methods.[2]

This article aims to provide a way forward for studies of the child, distinct from that indicated by Lee Edelman's book *No Future: Queer Theory and the Death Drive* (2004). In this work, Edelman turns a psychoanalytic lens on the figure of the child as it appears in English literature including Charles Dickens and George Eliot, and eviscerates the notion of "reproductive futurity" anchored around the "universal" modernist tropes of child raising that configure infancy as a limiting force and engine of dependency, protection, discipline, education, and vulnerability. Edelman counters this with an equally universal, psychoanalytic notion of queer sexuality that rejects redemptive or reproductive futurity and developmentalist teleologies while embracing unintelligibility, negativity, *jouissance*, and the psychoanalytic notion of the death drive. Although it is not Edelman's intention, his book's focus on "the" universal, ideal figuration of "the Child" risks repositioning figurations of childness (and, even more forcefully, the heteronormative parent) as "infantile" and as quintessential objects or vehicles of security practices. The infantilism of reproductive futurity comes to stand in as the universalized opposite of queer potentiality, creativity, and subversion. This may lead the reader to deduce that youthful agency, as realized by actual children in particular locations, histories, or struggles, tends to push back or drag down forms of subversive or resistant praxis. I worry that Edelman's (2004: 139) embrace of "unintelligibility," attached to rejection of the "Child" and its "world-making logic of heterosexual meaningfulness" throws out the baby with the bathwater (you knew that metaphor was coming!). Can we afford to abandon questions of legibility if we are to challenge normative infantilization and developmentalist futurism? Are noninfantile and nonsecuritizing "children's politics" only intelligible as "playfulness" and not as "real" politics? Or have we just ignored the histories, languages, practices, and collective formations that render these practices legible and that reveal the political seriousness of children's playfulness?

In response to these particular questions, this article provides a public ethnography and social history of "children" as collective political, cultural, and economic actors in a particular context where their assertions have been wildly consequential but strangely unremarked by either queer or conventional scholarship. I take the political "play" of children seriously here to the degree that it is hardly recognizable as play. As an analytical experiment, I hypothesize that this playful character of action and expression is determined not by these political actors' age or immaturity but by their social, material, and historical conditions and by their shared, transferred and accumulated experience. Thus I suspend the exceptionalism of traditional child studies that takes as a starting point the savage or natural or undisciplined, blank-slate character of "childish" behavior. Instead I argue that this identification of children in particular contexts with aspects of control, enforcement, objects of emergency protection (thus, as hubs of "securitization") is historically and sociospatially specific. Infantilization, or the naturalization of this process as anchored to apprehension and protection of "children," involves a specific set of political logics that are not psychoanalytically constant or universal but in fact deeply contested, materially, culturally, socially, and institutionally. I demonstrate that although our ways of seeing block the legibility of child agency, "children" are actively engaged in collective and contingent ways in confronting and reversing these processes of securitization and infantilization.

Methodologically, this article combines political-economic history, cultural studies, and political anthropology of the state and state-linked media. I develop a method based on the specific conventions of "public ethnography," and I strictly avoid the one-on-one approaches of "participant observation" and the limitations of interview or survey-based methods. My perspective benefits from my having lived in Egypt for eight years in extended periods between 1990 and 2014, where I resided in densely populated working-class neighborhoods in Cairo that served as manufacturing and market hubs, where child labor and childcentric street economies are commonplace. At regular intervals during these periods, the buildings, squares, schools, and transport hubs in the zones where I lived have been swept up in wave after wave of children's collective celebration, protest, expression, disruption, and occupation. But the prerogatives of the local state as well as global social science norms make it difficult to render legible these practices or to record their voices. Interviews with very young activists, workers, and organizers are not possible in the context of state and sexual violence against children, severe repression of academic freedom, prohibitions on child labor, and, in Egypt, the criminalization as treasonous and perverted of any "collaboration with children" that can be seen as fostering resistance to the state. Additionally, the human-subjects review norms of contemporary social science in the United States require that an interview subject be twenty-one years of age or have participation and consent of a parent.

With these critical problems in mind, this article builds on three sets of innovative conversations at the intersection of child studies and queer studies. First, I build on brilliant notions of "the wild" in relation to "failed" youth and queer children as articulated in Jack Halberstam's *Queer Art of Failure* (2011) and an unpublished 2013 work, and in the last lectures of the late José Esteban Muñoz (2012). Second, I am inspired by outstanding recent work on the "invention" of the queer child as vividly reimagined in the work of Kathryn Bond Stockton (2009), the class and gender-marked child configured through spectacular anxieties as analyzed by Cindi Katz (2008) and Eli Zaretsky (1976), and the global categories of adolescent and youth as revealed in the research of Philippe Ariès (1962) and Edward Shorter (1975). Third, I offer my own spin on conversations around "unruly politics," although I want to be careful to remain anchored in contentious histories, social/racial structures, and cultural practices, and not lean toward romanticism.

In this case study of Egypt, I demonstrate that children are an active political force and that their participation, inspiration, and particular mobilization tactics were crucial in the lead-up to the January 25 Revolution of 2011 (also referred to as the Tahrir Square uprisings) as well as in the authoritarian backlash that characterized the post-2013 period. Children's politics differ from those of "youth" or adults in the terms of their "playfulness" (a term that I substantially resignify here), queering logics, carnivalesque temporalities, and materialization in certain spaces, infrastructures, and settings. I offer a specific cultural-political contextualization for the carnivalesque and the infrastructure of children's insurgency that is distinct from the ideal-typical designation of the carnivalesque developed by Mikhail Bakhtin (1984) and interrogates directly the orientalist fantasy of unruly sensuality (Chouiten 2012) that is reproduced, unironically, by the "children's perversity" discourse of the Egyptian security apparatus. Through a materially grounded cultural-political analysis, my aim is to demonstrate that despite their political activities, extraordinary public and collective visibility, and extensive participation in the labor force, children are forcibly misrecognized as not having political force with agency and agenda.

These issues become particularly urgent in a time when masses of "child" workers, culture makers, and political militants (who are seen as criminally perverse and politically treacherous specifically because they have been categorized as children) have emerged as some of the most powerful and disruptive collective actors in social uprisings and street occupations in the Middle East, South Asia, and Latin America since 2008. Does the fact that these workers and militants are between six and sixteen years of age mean that they cannot mobilize against infantilization? It seems it is their destiny to do so.

In this context, this study turns to Egypt, to turn inside out the global politics of securitized infantilization that is animated by the contemporary set of symbolic and geopolitical process that Stockton, in this issue, refers to as "kid orientalism." This study includes three sections that present three case studies. These case studies in turn provide three theoretical frameworks for thinking about children and infantilization in Egypt and across the globe. First is emancipatory *inhiraf* and labor agency, a theory that rescripts queer questions of agency around the Arabic term *inhiraf*, which signifies both the *perversion* of the street as contested public space of gender/class struggles and social pluralization, and the *deviance* of the child who slips out of the space of the family and timeline of maturation. Second is child sovereignties and 'Eid temporalities, a claim that those subjectified as "children" merit majority status as they mount collective challenges to practices of infantilization in the realm of work, sexuality, and politics. Third is Ultra-generational tactics and wild disinfantilization, a mapping of the mass-mobilizing activities of very young workers, street denizens, and football/soccer fan collectives who are labeled "Ultras" in Egypt. These Ultra tactics I further disaggregate into three sets of child-mobilized expressions: *the swarming of child-labor circuits* and spaces identified with child work, vending, and public sociability; *the repacing of flows of futurity* by interrupting, strolling/dragging, clogging the pace of operation of infrastructures of consumption and commuting; and *the imposition of* 'efreet *sovereignty in carnivalesque temporalities*, drawing on the "little trickster demon" symbolic figure ("'efreet" in Egyptian Arabic) to generate the alternative routes to recognize child sexuality, claims to rule, and acts of redistribution.

Egypt's "Brazilian Solution" and Global Children's Movements

On June 19, 2014, the once-progressive Egyptian newspaper *Al-Masry Al-Youm* published a distressing editorial. The author, Nassar Abdullah, a poet and professor of moral philosophy at Sohag University in Egypt, argued that his government should adopt what he called "the Brazilian Solution":

> In the 1990s, street children in Brazil's major towns turned from a source
> of annoyance to a source of terror, increasingly committing crimes includ-
> ing rape, prostitution, and murder, while the economic situation of Brazil
> was similar to Egypt's present condition. . . . Thus the Brazilian security
> forces unleashed a campaign to hunt down and kill the street children
> like stray dogs, to avoid the dangers. . . . That harsh solution managed to
> cleanse the streets of major cities in Brazil from street children. It hap-
> pened because the political leadership had the will to reform and to fight
> corruption as well as provide jobs. This is the lesson everyone should learn
> from the Brazilian experience. (*Ahram Online* 2014)

Though Abdullah's mercilessly moral-authoritarian approach to street children represents a drastic change from recent Egyptian policy, the fact that he was inspired by Brazil is no surprise, as security state institutions in Egypt and Brazil have had a long history of exchanging ideas and practices. In the 1990s both countries engaged in similar practices to secure UN summit mega-events: the Rio Conference on the Environment in 1992 and the Cairo Conference on Population in 1994. At the time, Egyptian intellectuals widely rejected the Candelaria Massacre of 1993, in which Brazilian militarized police exterminated fifty street children, and Egypt's child-welfare authorities stood wholly against such brutality. In fact, in the 1990s, Egypt pioneered in a radically demilitarized, nonmoralistic approach to "street children" that explicitly diverged from that of Brazil. This policy redefined the subject of the child in relation to humanitarian interventions by rehabilitating the reputation of "the street" as a space of agency for children rather than a cradle of deviancy, and by shedding light on the home as a space of domestic violence and child exploitation rather than of "protection" alone. The Egyptian sociologist Kamal Fahmi (2007: 11), drawing on more than eight years of urban fieldwork in Cairo in the 1990s and early 2000s, wrote of Egypt's street children: "Far from being mere victims or deviants, these children, in running away from alienating home lives and finding relative freedom in the street, are capable of actively defining their situations in their own terms. They are able to challenge the roles assigned to children, make judgments, and develop a network of niches

and resources in a teeming metropolis such as Cairo. . . . Social workers and others need to respect the agency the children display in changing their own lives."
Fahmi's pro-empowerment movement worked in solidarity with children rather
than securitizing and "protecting" them. Thus he demonstrated the possibility for
challenging the relationship between humanitarian intervention and the discourse
of the home/family as disciplinary agency of the state.

But Fahmi's set of empowering alternatives were violently supplanted
starting in the early 2000s, as the figure of "street children" increasingly became
an obsession of state security's intensifying operations in Egypt. Securing child
sexuality became crucial to a state effort to relegitimize the police, framing them
as moral agents whose efforts to control the street would restore discipline to society as a whole. The sexuality of street children became a symbolic node in state
efforts to solve larger social and economic problems. Popular discourses like that
of the "marriage crisis" linked countrywide economic issues to local concerns
about whether working- and middle-class men would be able to afford to marry
(Hasso 2010). The "marriage crisis" proposed that the Egyptian state should rescue a certain family structure that would, in turn, unleash jobs and economic
growth somehow. In this context, any politics that recognized children as agents
became framed as a sex crime (Nader 2016), an act of terror that, by refusing to
structurally adjust the family in crisis, threatened this one fragile avenue of socio-
economic transformation.

By 2014, as evidenced by Abdullah's editorial cited above, this protective
discourse of family rescue was twinned with a brutal punitive project, supporting
the arrest, torture, and detention, and even extermination, of children protesting
in or occupying streets and public thoroughfares. This, commenters like Abdullah dared to argue, would not just "cleanse" the city: it would somehow unleash
job growth; purge Egyptian society of AIDS, prostitution, and sexual predation;
launch what they saw as a Brazil-style economic boom; and even build a demo-
cratic state purged of corruption. These were not only the recommendations of
military or police leaders. As cited above, radical policy recommendations against
children even appeared in the writing of a professor of moral philosophy, himself
deeply self-identified with a humane project for the state.

On January 25, 2014, during the three-year anniversary of the popular uprisings that centered on Tahrir Square—called in Egypt "the January 25
Revolution"—children appeared in Tahrir Square and in front of the court building where deposed president Mohamed Morsi was standing trial. Several children,
ages six to nine, were holding large black military boots on their head, or wore
them as hats, tied to their heads with string around their chins. These children

stood alongside parents who were holding posters supporting General Abdel Fattah al-Sisi and asking him to run for president (AbdelAzim 2014). By strapping boots to their heads, these children expressed support for military rule, for repression, for the stomping out of political and civil liberties.[3]

Three months later, at the end of April, another kind of militarized child grabbed headlines in Egypt. Fleeing domestic abuse by a brutal father, a thirteen-year-old boy fled his home and began living with a group of friends that orbited around child-empowerment NGOs in downtown Cairo. The father eventually tracked down his son at "Al-Balady," a social-educational organization in downtown Cairo that shelters "street children" from abuse, offers them counseling, and mobilizes civil groups around issues of stopping sexual harassment and advocating children's rights (Mazidi 2014). When the father found his son participating in the children's rights organization, he called in his friends from the State Security directorate and plainclothes thugs linked to the police. They invaded the NGO and brutally assaulted and detained several children, as well as the cofounder of the organization, Aya Hegazy, a university professor and children's rights specialist. As reported by Hegazy's mother, Hosny:

> Hegazy was interrogated by National Security and was hit on the neck in the process. "It made her fall to her knees. The officer called her names and said he would urinate in her vagina and that she should be sentenced to death, or at least to a life sentence." . . . She added that another officer asked her to confess that she has been receiving foreign funds and that she has been deceived, in order to prompt her release. The Interior Ministry released a statement regarding the arrests, claiming the children taken by police from the organization testified that they had been paid by the defendants to participate in protests and instructed to sexually assault each other, in order to make it hard for them to return to their families. . . . only four out of the 21 children arrested in the raid [and certainly tortured to force confessions] testified against the four defendants. (Masr 2014)

Ten years before, an organization in Cairo run by Kamal Fahmi—the sociologist studying street children cited above—was raided and disbanded. As in that case, "Al-Balady" was accused of turning children into queer sex predators and into soldiers against the state, merely by giving them space to express themselves and to develop on their own terms more equitable sociabilities.

Dominant contemporary Egyptian representations tend to present children in contentious street politics as engines of extreme affect rather than as social subjects with histories, interests, and agendas. As Edelman (2004) contends, children also serve as visual shorthands for ideologically overburdened metaphors like "risk" and "futurity," which haunt us with what is lacking or fragile in the political present or social structure. When children are seen in these cases, they are hypervisible while being sociopolitically inapprehensible. They are seen everywhere in images of emergency journalism without being perceived, recognized, or engaged on their own terms as political actors or social claims-makers. Perhaps children are hard to recognize as political actors not just because of infantilization but also because of how the very specific category of youth functions. Youth, in the discourse of modernity, in both colonial and its anticolonial forms, seems to stand proudly on the threshold of more fresh, more modern, and more idealistic adulthood. In Western representations of the Arab Spring, the youth stands as an iconic figuration of the liberalized, modernized, moderate adult-in-waiting, a class of tech-savvy, middle-class, secular cosmopolitan aspirants. As El Shakry (2011) has eloquently argued, the modern category of youth emerged in Egypt in the 1940s within a particular set of projects. At this time, the figure of youth was abstracted from particular geographies of social life and regional practices. Youth became resignified as a distinct "stage of development." El Shakry writes that in the 1940s, "adolescence—perceived as both a collective temporality and a depoliticized individual interiority—became a volatile stage linked to a psychoanalytic notion of sexuality as libidinal raw energy" (591). Yet in the current context, there are many indications that the "child" has become a distinct epistemological category rivaling "youth" in political importance, in Egypt and across the Arab region, but whose political sovereignty and legitimacy is constantly unrecognizable because of the intersecting apparatuses of securitization and infantilization. Since the 1990s, children in general, but particularly those seen as "loose children" or street children, have become identified as a collective reservoir of dangerously concentrated libidinal energy. In the optic of securitization processes, public discourse and policing practices have designated the "child" as a category that is less interior and less psychologically contained than that of "youth." Children are figured as embedded in certain street spaces, socially contentious geographies, and dissident practices that challenge the depoliticizing containment fields of the psychoanalytic or therapeutic, and trigger full mobilization of the violence of the human-security state rather than the redistributive apparatus of a welfare state or the kind of revolutionary governance proposed by the 2011 uprising. Through a discussion of children's movements in Egypt leading up to the 2011 uprising, the next section analyzes children's activism and how it operates as the other of this liberal youth that operated as the dominant celebratory framing of the original phase of the Arab Spring, as well as the Other of the kid Orientalism of the new humanitarian discourse of the west.

In global resistance movements, children act as self-organized subjects of unruly politics as well as manipulated objects of authoritarian populism. Representations of seemingly new forms of childcentric mass politics and collective actions invoke scampering embodiment, carnivals of play and cruelty, swarming interruptions and derailing circulations. "Children" are less likely than "youth" to be protesting or engaging in formal sit-ins, less interested in marching, but more engaged in bursting out of detention and the institutions that warehouse them, or in swarming through the pristine spaces of safety and containment—including soccer stadiums and shopping zones—in which elite adults have shuttered themselves. But I argue here that these practices of interrupting flows and imposing *'efreet* forms of child sovereignty through carnivalesque temporalities derive not from the playfulness or ludic or libidinous nature of this "stage" in development but from particular social histories, cultural geographies, and circulating global tactics.

Emancipatory *Inhiraf* and Labor Agency

Since the 1990s, global movements advocating the empowerment of street children have demanded decriminalization and confronted policing strategies that designate children as an inherently perverse and criminal category. Emerging in the 1990s and early 2000s in Egypt, India, and Colombia, these child-empowerment movements offered a strongly agency-centric approach to the problem of street children. Many academic works have contributed to children's empowerment movements, including Lewis Aptekar's (1989) book on Colombian street children in Santiago de Cali, Iman Bibars's (1998) discussion of street children in Egypt that demands an end to punitive and carceral responses, N. H. Hussein's (2003) arguments about the resilient cultural and social formations self-generated by children normally considered the most vulnerable, and Sheela Patel's (1990) book on street children's resilience in Bombay.

Unique to Egyptian scholarship on street children is an insistence on refusing paternalizing victimization discourse, and a critique of the romanticism that characterizes some of the Andean and South Asian literature of the 1990s and 2000s that may verge into a neoliberal celebration of children's bootstrapping self-help practices and entrepreneurial autonomy from the state. Nelly Ali, a bold and articulate Egyptian children's rights activist who emerged from this movement, has researched the particular social coping strategies and child-generated cultural and spatial practices that allow for maximum resilience. Her work on street children recommends recognizing their "exceptional fortitude" (Ali 2011: 260) and mobilizing resources to enable their agency while asking for particular state interventions and changes to public provisions of health, housing, and educational aid to street children.

This dual approach of demanding aid and valorizing child autonomy responds to Egyptian law, which categorizes autonomous children as *Mu'arid lil-Inhiraf* ("liable to perversion"), defining street children through a discourse of vulnerability. Police record-keeping creates registries of vulnerable children, ostensibly to map populations requiring care, yet "children in police custody face beatings [and] sexual abuse" (Human Rights Watch 2003b). On July 25, 2003, Human Rights Watch released a report, "Charged with Being Children," detailing "abuses during arrest, transport, and in lockups" and recommending "immediately ending [the] practice of arresting children considered 'vulnerable to delinquency,' or 'vulnerable to danger' and amend[ing] Child Law 12 of 1996 to ensure that no child is penalized for 'status offenses,' that is, conduct that would not be penalized if committed by an adult" (Human Rights Watch 2003a: 4–5). Thus, the Egyptian practice of marking autonomous children as vulnerable "protects" children by policing them.

Laws seeming to protect street children can be especially pernicious in this regard. Egypt's controversial "Child Law" of 2001 mandated access to food, bedding, and medical care for street children, empowering police to provide these resources by detaining and charging children, since the law considered more than 25 percent of Egypt's children "vulnerable to perversion/delinquency." Thus, as a representative instrument of what I call "the human-security state," the law criminalized its subjects as it protected them. A 2011 study by the Egyptian government's National Center for Social and Criminological Research (which informs the state's social intervention agendas as well as policing priorities) reported that "at least 20% of street children [are] victims of trafficking, mostly for sexual exploitation; and are also involved in theft, and in the sale of narcotics" (IOM 2011: 17). The concept of child vulnerability, as expressed in Egyptian law and government discourse, implies that the children of the urban popular classes are, in general, a criminal class. Like colonial humanitarian agencies of the early twentieth century, contemporary human-security state formations in Egypt identify notions of vulnerability with liability, perversity, deviance, and delinquency. Under the label *Mu'arid lil-Inhiraf*, children's vulnerability makes them personally and collectively liable, both in the sense that they are seen as likely to be perverted, deviant, or delinquent in their behavior and that they are made criminally responsible. Because street children are seen as both legally responsible for their behavior and likely to commit criminal acts, these children can be policed en masse. Because children who are removed from the family are seen as liable to perversion, police may deploy forms of brutal detention, punishment, sexual abuse, and forced labor against street children in order to protect an imagined notion of childhood innocence. The humanitarian discourse of international aid agencies, even as it insistently stands against police abuse in its campaigns to raise awareness (and raise money), dovetails with the human-security state's discourse of the child as a self-prostituting deviant requiring supervision. UNICEF's 2000 report on Egypt stated: "These children lead an unhealthy and often dangerous life that leaves them deprived of their basic needs for protection, guidance, and supervision and exposes them to different forms of exploitation and abuse. For many, survival on the street means begging and sexual exploitation by adults" (13).

The process of counting the number of "street children"—often defined as those who are autonomous from families and who have no viable or acceptable relatives from which to draw support—reveals how this status category of mass vulnerability is invented even as it functions. During the 1990s, when Egyptian activists were challenging the production of these criminalized status categories, individuals were carefully counted, and so the official total of street children was a more modest sum. In 1999 the Egyptian government counted 17,228 street children in the entire country of Egypt. Then in June 2009, "The NCCM [National Council for Childhood and Motherhood] snapshot survey counted 12,000 street living children and street-working children in Greater Cairo" (Farrag 2013: 5). The Greater Cairo population since 2009 has approached 20 million, or about 20 percent of the country's entire population. But by 2011, when the discourse of child criminality had gained more power, the Egyptian government counted three million street children in Cairo, alone. These number counts vary wildly in relation to Egypt's total population, which approached one hundred million by 2014. Are street children a subsector of the homeless population numbering in the thousands, or are "street children" to be equated with an entire generation of unruly children of the poor, 25 percent of the young population, who are officially "liable" for criminality, perversity, and repression? The Egyptian journalist and children's rights activist Amira El Feky (2013) writes:

> It is easy for us to categorize and label street children. To us, they are ruthless criminals, beggars, the puppets of unknown forces, drug addicts or miserable victims. . . . Ironically, NGOs and individuals who work with street children or advocate for their rights largely stick to those same labels. Instead of condemning what the street children do, however, they . . .

address our compassion with heart-breaking stories. These stories are true and heart-breaking but it is questionable whether telling them serves the goal of advocating street children's rights or if they merely serve to "raise awareness."

The resort to horror as "awareness" is tied to the inability to recognize children as workers. One reason that children are forced into the status category of the vulnerable, liable, and perverse—requiring security responses rather than legitimizing empowerment and redistribution—is because of the taboo around recognizing the reality of child labor. UNICEF presented data that "boys and girls between the ages of six and eleven make up about one quarter of children who work in Egypt" (UNICEF Egypt 2004). In July 2011, a report jointly produced by the International Labor Organization and the Egyptian Center for Statistics and Planning found 1.6 million children laborers in Egypt (about 10 percent of the total workforce) (ILO/CAPMAS 2012). This report acknowledged that the real total may be far greater, since children tend to work in informal businesses or off-the-record apprenticeships or agricultural labor. Furthermore, this total counted only those under the age of thirteen, since Egyptian law permits children aged fourteen to eighteen to work legally. Taking these other groups into account, "children" may make up 50 percent of the workforce of Egypt's most difficult jobs. As the ILO/CAPMAS report makes clear: "A whopping 82 per cent (1.32 million) of total underage workers work in adverse conditions, which includes exhausting jobs, exposure to dust, smoke, high or low temperatures, chemicals, insecticides, and so forth. . . . 29 per cent work more than 43 hours a week, more than 8 hours daily in a 5-day work week" (quoted in Feteha 2011).

Since 2011, child labor has been on the rise (*Albawaba* 2011). State violence against children also rose dramatically during this period, even as the state-security discourse generated constant moral panic around the need to save the nation's children from the threat of violence and instability. In January 2013 Ultras soccer fan clubs and other children's and young people's movements were visible leading their own protests and in clashes with police. As Alastair Beach (2013) reported, "In the wake of the [January 2013 clashes] which left scores of people dead, hundreds of children have been illegally detained by the Egyptian police. Many of them have been beaten, tortured, and sexually humiliated by their captors." Beach quotes Karim Ennarah, a researcher for the Cairo-based Egyptian Initiative for Personal Rights, who argues that the rate and severity of child detention over the past month is unprecedented:

> Numerous testimonies have reached rights workers and lawyers about children under 15 being held in both security camps and police cells prior to trial—a clear contravention of the Child Law, which states that minors cannot be held in police detention. . . . There have been numerous other reports of elementary-school-age youngsters being detained in police facilities. . . . At a press conference held by one NGO last week, a 12-year-old boy described how, after being arrested in downtown Cairo, he was stripped naked by a police lieutenant and forced to commit an "indecent act" in front of officers. (Beach 2013)

With such a large portion of Egypt's detainees and those abused by the security state, and with such a significant population of the workforce consisting of children—including a significant proportion of children under the age of twelve—working long hours, often in informal-sector occupations, and circulating between shops, vendors, villages, and streets, why should it be surprising that these individuals should have grievances and participate in protests against the current order?

During the revolutionary uprisings in Egypt in 2011–12, according to a report for *All Things Considered* (Nelson 2012), children "placed themselves on the front line. . . . Activists say several have been killed or wounded in recent months by gunfire and tear gas. Plus, 1 out of every 4 protesters thrown in jail following clashes in December was a child. Their advocates say most, if not all, of these kids live on Cairo's streets, and that they see the revolution as a way to escape their isolation from society." Nelson quotes Amira, a rally organizer in Cairo, who said, "The children are valuable partners in the Egyptian revolution given their speed, agility and small size, which make it harder for security forces to stop them." She added, "It is important to recognize their contribution, which is why she and a teen acquaintance organized the rally" (ibid.). In a subsequent news conference, "General Adel Emara accused activists he did not name of paying children and teens to throw rocks and Molotov cocktails at security forces. The general also showed a poor-quality video of a boy named Sami confessing to his interrogator that he received the equivalent of $33 to attack buildings. Many children's rights activists in Egypt suspect the confession was coerced. They accuse the generals of using the kids to try to discredit the pro-democracy movement and justify soldiers' use of deadly force" (ibid.).

As demonstrated above, human-security discourse, whether deployed by military agents of the state, or among liberals and progressives, tends to assume that children are being "used," forced, or "lured" into demonstrations. An article by

Jacob Lippincott of the *Week* (2013) typifies journalism that casts child activists as disempowered victims: "At the bottom end of Egypt's underclass are the countless homeless children who were cast out by impoverished parents. Packs of barefoot, filthy preadolescents are ubiquitous in central parts of Cairo, and are often drawn to street violence like moths to a flame, serving as stone-throwing cannon fodder for both the police and demonstrators." The discourse of child vulnerability also permeates political discourse. During the July–August 2013 sit-in by the Muslim Brotherhood in Rabaa al-Adawiya Square, which demanded the reinstatement of deposed President Morsi, the Brotherhood were accused of "using" children as human shields or propaganda, or trucking them in from orphanages. UNICEF warned of the illegality of deliberately putting children in danger (*Al Arabiya News* 2013). However, Egyptian children have their own social histories of taking over streets and asserting sovereignty, on their own terms, not just as lured or exploited by others in times of political uprising.

Child Sovereignties and 'Eid Temporalities

When they converge around the figure of the child, moral panics tend to compound each other and intersect, and the notion of the family and of humanity itself is resecuritized using infantilizing modes of panic and control. In this context, the figure of the street child recurs throughout the history of repression. But there is also an alternative subaltern social history of autonomous children's practices, celebrated by popular religiosity and urban festival culture in Egypt.

The notion of spatial areas and temporal periods in which children rule by performing spectacular forms of unruly or *'efreet* sovereignty is not a novelty in Egypt, not a reflection of some new collapse of discipline or crisis in family regulation, not an emergency of urban public modernity. Rather, regular episodes of "children's rule" or an "Empire of Children" are strongly identified with popular Egyptian religious festivities that take on a joyful, unruly, carnival-like character. The biggest of these festivities is 'Eid al-Fitr, the festival of the breaking of the fast that marks the end of the holy month of Ramadan. This 'Eid begins with a uniquely inclusive prayer gathering that does not segregate men from women. The ceremony brings everyone together—particularly to include young children in the prayer—loosening the norms of prayer, propriety, and gender in the process. If the family can afford it, children are often given new clothes, toys, balls, and gifts at this time. Most important, children are often ceded control over street spaces. During 'Eid al-Fitr, children from age seven through seventeen take over the streets to play games, taunt adults, play tricks on each other and their neighbors, and assert a vibrant and sometimes rather menacing form of rule. In the early evening hours, groups of girls or mixed-gender clusters rule the street together, but at night boys tend to take over, lording over these spaces until dawn and beyond.

Over centuries, as popular practices have proliferated and children's sovereignties have developed their own traditions accelerated by the transformation of 'Eid by consumer capitalism and street-vending economies, this moment of children's rule has stretched to last for four or five days. During these days, young children are loaned or given (or borrow or steal) bicycles, mopeds, even occasionally cars and mini-pickup trucks, and buzz around city streets at night, unleashed. Delivery boys, shop girls, mechanics' apprentices, little vegetable merchants from the country, and street vendor kids rule the urban economy during this time. Usually these children constitute over 50 percent of the labor in these urban merchant, vendor, small shop, and home-factory economies. However, during the days of 'Eid they act as the bosses, honchos, and thugs of these businesses—cartoon versions of the coercive adults who rule over their labor during the rest of the year. Cliques of boys aged eight to twelve can be seen strutting about, chain-smoking their cheap Cleopatra cigarettes, and evicting parents and shoppers from the sidewalk, establishing hegemony over outdoor cafés. The carousels, BB gun booths, and 'Arous (Punch and Judy) puppet shows pop and screech with childhood cruelty and glee throughout the nights. Much play around sexuality is infused in these times and spaces of children's rule (Ambrust 2002; Schielke and Winegar 2012; Schielke 2015; Winegar and Deeb 2015). Groups of young girls flirt boldly with young men, even grabbing them, and boys will catcall and grab at girls and young women. This environment of childhood flirtation has led to the depiction of 'Eid festivities by some media and by organs of the security state as a landscape of sexual assault, with children sexually preying on other children (Ambrust 2002).

'Eid al-Fitr is not the only time and space in which these forms of children's sovereignty are partially sacralized in the context of popular religious practices and social history and asserted by kids themselves. During Sufi Moulids, festivals surrounding revered members of the Prophet's family, or Sufi "saints," there is often a large degree of children's sovereignty in certain corners of the festivities. Of course, adults are in charge of operating sweet carts, *dhikr* tents, traveling circuses, magic shows, loop-the-loop iron rides, whirling carousels, and kazoo-screeching puppet shows. Sufi sheikhs also host more serious gatherings for devotional prayers and chanting of the dhikr. Street spaces, however, are flooded with children, groups of girls and boys, linked arm in arm, carousing and cruising and enjoying the space. Perhaps contrary to expectation, the number of children in the streets increases as night falls, and after midnight the streets are flooded with the noise and motion of thousands of children in these Moulids. Whereas children in 'Eid festivities may appear particularly proper, even wearing new clothes, at Moulids children and adolescents often cross-dress—though this has been policed and reduced in just the past years, as a new "tradition" of strict gender binarism has been invented and enforced by Salafist moral-panic campaigns. Nevertheless, six-year-old girls can still be seen wearing bushy fake black moustaches and tarboush ("fez") hats, while boys, like in the Moulid Carnival parade of Saeeda Aisha, will dress as belly dancers or women movie stars and dance frenetically on the parade floats, the donkey-led vegetable carts, or the shoebox delivery trucks.

These periods of "world upside down" in which children rule over an empire of play, reigning over street spaces and street economies, and in which children are aggressive, explicitly sexual, and gender-bending, mockingly authoritarian and anarchic at the same time, mark the intersection of popular nonorthodox religious tradition and carnivalesque Mediterranean festival culture. These street festivities also represent an explosion of trapped energies, after children and families have been contained every night by long, late Ramadan dinners where the domestic family sphere is concentrated and celebrated to the point of exhaustion. Festivals like 'Eid and Sufi Moulids are traditionally viewed as moments of celebration of the child as special beneficiary of family piety, generosity, and love. However, from a child's perspective, they are also times of joyful revelry in the nondomestic, nonfamily forms of sociability, commerce, modes of circulation, and encounter. These are utopian moments, but often threatening and violent ones as children unleash cruelty and even sexual aggression on adults and each other, as the child labor that constitutes sometimes the majority of lower-middle-class and working-class urban and peri-urban economies gets to enact its assumption of particular kinds of sovereignty. Festivals of child sovereignty may also be seen as a form of protest through occupation, as the streets represent a more "real" public space to child workers than the vast squares identified as symbolic public spaces by protesters.

The politics of these festivals has shifted since the 1990s, with the rise of Salafist public morality vigilantism, and with the infiltration of street publics by plainclothes "security agents" who are formed and contracted by rich merchants as well as by the Interior Ministry, and who deploy explicitly sexually assaultive forms of social control.[4] In 1995 a moral panic coalesced around children's transvestism during Moulid parades. Salafists, in league with President Hosni Mubarak's culture ministry, raged against the vulgarity and moral abomination of Moulids, leaving Sufi leaders at Al-Azhar stuck in between. In the discourse of this moral panic, children came to embody the most vulgar and morally abominable figures. In 2005–9, the Egyptian press began to argue for what it called a state security threat around "children's rule during 'Eid al-Fitr, as a problem of working-class unruliness, and as a cathexis of the so-called marriage crisis and the crisis of the Egyptian family.

As social control over 'Eids and Moulids began to descend, mobilizations for "children's sovereignty" exploded beyond the designated times and spaces of popular religiosity and carnivalesque Sufi and Ramadan festivities, and asserted themselves in new times and places. Children's militancy began in the late 1990s, but increased in frequency and intensity in the years leading up to the 2011 uprisings. Drawing from and often invoking the carnivalesque logics of Moulids and 'Eid festivities, but breaking out of the "exceptionalist" box of the Ramadan/Moulid religious calendar, children began to take over other spaces and interrupt specific modes of circulation. In 2009 and 2010, in several cases children in Egypt took over their primary schools, evicting teachers and the state. These incidents responded to shifts in Egyptian education since the 1990s, when President Mubarak signed a stringent accord with the International Monetary Fund that utterly dismantled the public school system, having massive effects on gender, class, generation, and space in schools.

Egyptian children have economic interests of their own. As laborers, they have familiarity with and mastery over particular spaces and modes of circulation. Egypt also has a rich religious and social history of children's sovereignty during festivals and 'Eids, while Egyptian children have more recent histories of channeling these 'Eid and Moulid modes of unruly sovereignty into the occupation of schools and street-commerce zones. From the perspective of the state, these extensions of children's sovereignty have been seen as a threat of sexual harassment or rape or a breakdown in family structures that can be fixed by Salafist morality brigades or police violence. However, child militants can also be seen as savvy activists, with claims of sovereignty and rights to the city, who assert demands for a greater share of economic revenue and a broader form of social and political power.

Spongy Presentism versus Arrested Futurism

Just as the mustachioed white Guy Fawkes mask of *V for Vendetta* became the iconic face of revolutionary Arab youth since 2011, SpongeBob SquarePants stands unchallenged as the superstar of children's rebellion and children's playful sovereignty in Egypt and across the Arab world. Emblazoned on schoolboys' T-shirts and shopgirls' headscarves, inserted into online memes, featured in graffiti murals, and invading political cartoons, "Sponge" has been deployed by Arab children to embody the spirit of political rebellion as well as the fun of unruliness with increasing frequency since 2012 (Berger 2013). If V is the avenging angel of justice representing youth against the repressive police state, then Sponge is the tricky demon of infantile disorder, ideological implosion, familyless sociability, sexual and bodily amorphousness, and most important, of boldly fearless playfulness.

The name of this cartoon antihero is rich in how it resonates in Egyptian colloquial dialect and in Cairene street slang. In Egypt, Mr. SquarePants is usually referred to just as Sponge (pronounced *sbinch*). SpongeBob is sometimes called "Pop," since Pop or Bob—interchangeable because of the play between the letter "b" and "p" in Arabic—is also an Egyptian children's street slang for "buddy." Sometimes, in a fun way, the colloquial pronunciation of "sponge/sbinch" morphs into "sbinkis," or Sphinx, a kitsch figure of Pharoanic nationalism in Egypt that formal Arabic refers to as Abu al-Huul. Sponge can also be pronounced "sfing," which is the literal term for sponge itself—the thing with which you wash dishes or polish shoes, or the foam pad on which you sleep when you are not out on the street.

But SpongeBob is also occasionally referred to as "Al-'Efreet"—the little demon. *'Efreet*, in the popular idiom of non-Orthodox Islam and in Sufi spiritualism, are the trickster jinni ("genie") figures and little devils that bring bad luck, tempt fate, plant deviant desires, and inspire love, lust, and rebellion. They resemble to some extent the darker, archaic notion of the fairy or fae people that animate Celtic lore. When children in Egypt throw obviously faked tantrums, or display gender-deviant or socially embarrassing behavior, Egyptian parents affectionately chide their children: "What a horrible little *'efreet!*" In a time of moral conservatism in which representations of popular nonorthodox religiosity are attacked by Salafist preachers and *amr maarouf* (well-known command) morality vigilante brigades—and where the women who channeled the presence of jinni and *'efreet* in spiritual ceremonies and during Zaar ecstatic gatherings have been charged with witchcraft and repressed—Sponge has snuck back to reanimate this spirit of the popular trickster. SpongeBob's winking, dancing form hangs from taxi drivers' rearview mirrors and is painted on the neighborhood walls where the blue Hand of Fatima might have been seen in the recent past.

Of course SpongeBob is not a native icon of childhood that emerges directly from any tradition in Egypt, although it does resonate with popular jinni culture and Sufi Islamic spiritualism. His origins are American, and his routes of transmission are those of consumer capitalism. SpongeBob was originally created by the artist Stephen Hillenburg, a trained marine biologist from Anaheim, California, who specializes in the life forms that dwell in intertidal pools. SpongeBob is, moreover, the intellectual property of Viacom Inc., a US-based transnational corporation. Viacom's diverse and often offbeat properties include *Dora the Explorer*, MTV's *Jersey Shore*, Logo's *RuPaul's Drag Race* characters, and Stephen Colbert's satirical conservative talk-show-host persona. Yet it would be incredibly simplistic to reduce the meaning of SpongeBob's ubiquity to the generic power of American consumer neoliberal capitalism—even as an instrument of Viacom's weirdo, queer-friendly, youth-slanted branch of consumer capitalism. More aggressively marketed figures of neoliberal consumer capitalism—Spider-Man, the Transformers, Batman, *My Little Pony*, Disney's Princesses franchise, Minecraft, and the inescapable empire of LEGO—have secured almost no place in the street cultures and carnival imaginaries of Egypt's children's movements. Those mainstream cartoon heroes and toy brandings do not seem to channel anything like SpongeBob's mass identification and connotation of rebellious joy in Egypt. His resonance to Arab Spring countries can be compared to American popular trickster figures like Br'er Rabbit or Bugs Bunny, and queer European diabolical figures like the Mad Hatter or Rumpelstiltskin.

If we do want to read SpongeBob as Western, then he lives in an explicitly post-American landscape, where the United States becomes a lost Atlantis sunk deep underwater (deep in debt? flooded by climate change?). Gender and race biopolitics have not been washed away but have been mushed and dissolved into an invertebrates-only habitat where Sponge constantly, accidentally, playfully, cruelly, stupidly undermines the ambition of the one form of capital—the Krabby Patty burger sold at a sunken 1950s-era diner, the Krusty Krab—and constantly inadvertently, playfully, fearlessly decimates the plans of the one would-be property owner, Squidward (Petersen 2013; Kingsley 2013). Jack Halberstam (2011: 1–2) discusses SpongeBob's anticapitalist leanings in *The Queer Art of Failure*, asking,

> What if, like SpongeBob SquarePants, we don't believe that a trip to the land of milk and honey inevitably ends at the gift shop? What is the alternative, in other words, to cynical resignation on the one hand and naïve optimism on the other? What is the alternative, SpongeBob wants to know, to working all day for Mr. Krabs, or being captured in the net of commodity capitalism while trying to escape? This book, a kind of "SpongeBob SquarePants Guide to Life," loses the idealism of hope in order to gain wisdom and a new spongy relation to life, culture, knowledge and pleasure.

In 2011 SpongeBob was explicitly targeted as a queer object of childhood subversion as well as cultural perversion. Salafist preachers in Kuwait, looking toward children's fan cultures in Egypt, demanded a fatwa against SpongeBob, arguing that he was a "perversion" that "acted like a girl" and threatened the Islamic family structure. This mirrored a 2005 controversy in which the US evangelical group Focus on the Family accused SpongeBob of "advocating homosexuality" (Associated Press 2005; BBC News 2005). In Egypt, opposition to Sponge-Bob came not just from the right wing: in 2013 the liberal satirist and popular TV host Bassem Youseff—who is all-too-often referred to as "the John Stewart of Egypt"—decried SpongeBob as reflecting the lack of locally produced, Egyptian-authentic children's literature, representing the corruption and consumerism of the once-proud Egyptian Revolutionary spirit. Yet SpongeBob's queer and, well, spongy embodiment of the spirit of children's rebellion is difficult to capture through any one category of power or to identify with any ideology or project of domination—certainly not the local/authentic versus the imperial/consumerist. Moreover, even groups who decry SpongeBob may be subject to his allure. On August 8, 2013, Sponge held a live pep rally, along with his purple buddy Barney and Shaun the Sheep, to cheer up children among the Muslim Brotherhood protesters sequestered in Rabaa al-Adawiya Square. Although the Salafists had declared Sponge queer and *haram* (religiously or morally forbidden), Brotherhood-affiliated entertainers took on the characters of Barney and SpongeBob, dressing up in colorful furry suits to sing.

While the figure of the street is always already laden with repressive and stigmatizing queer meaning when married to the figure of the child, "the Sponge" has picked up on popular non-Orthodox religiosity, children's *'efreet* culture, and the "kids sovereignty" of 'Eid celebrations. Images of SpongeBob symbolically mark the street as a landscape of little devils and tricksters, and a playful, post-American transcendence of the religious-secular divide, all while displacing questions of gender. A sponge is an undeveloped body, invertebrate, satirically cruel but not hard or orthodox, not muscular or gendery or curvy. SpongeBob is a subject best suited to winking and sticking out his tongue, flirty not lusty. Bob, or Pop, is a figure of the spongy present that will not submit to adult embodiment or orthodox norms; "he" is not a body that represents the arrested development of a future. The embrace of SpongeBob embraces a pleasure in the present, not complacent presentism wallowing in "stability" but a playful moment-focus that likes the unruly, the overturned, the interrupted as a form of play. This is the kind of childhood that infantilization discourse describes as "arrested development."

Ultra-Generational Tactics and Wild Disinfantilization

While SpongeBob represents the *'efreet* dynamics of serious play and the substantive world-making of specific carnivalesque cultural economies, young sports culture offers an explicit case of antistate organization. Egyptian soccer (football) fan clubs have emerged since the late 1990s as a unique form of collective organization and coordination among children and teenagers. These well-organized cheering clubs and youth collectivities—called "Ultras" in colloquial Arabic, English, and in many other languages including Italian, German, and Brazilian Portuguese—are not unique to Egypt. However, these soccer clubs have distinct identities within each country in terms of their social class profile, political leanings, relationship to other populist or popular mobilizations, and whether they include girls and young women as participants and leaders. In some countries, Ultras lean to the political Right and dovetail with skinhead groups or hooligans. In most countries, however, Ultras are made up of younger members whose adolescent or prepubescent bodies do not threaten the violence stereotypically associated with the coursing testosterone of a "hooligan's" body. When they are children's fan groups, Ultras reject physical violence and intimidation and instead employ mass coordination, vulgar chanting, and rhythmic collective expressions. These Ultra mass movements take place in stadiums during games or in street protests; they may even interrupt highways, metro lines, or government motorcades.

Ultras may even be seen as early instigators of the Egyptian Revolution. In important ways, the Ultras—movements largely among children, adolescents, and teenagers—generated key resistance tactics and created public momentum against the corporate oligarchization of sports and public space in general, against both the media's star system and their moral panics, and against the repressive apparatus of the police state. These movements were crucial in the years leading up to the 2011 uprisings, though they remain invisible in accounts that focus on their big sisters and brothers in the "Facebook generation," or on labor, youth, and student movements. Ultras were also some of the first civilians to be arrested and tried in military tribunals during this time, since they were arrested for being unruly in arenas owned by military officers. This set a precedent for the current logic of repression whereby any action taken near "military-owned" property—including stadiums, shopping malls, highways, public buildings, and dozens of other forms of property and infrastructure—can justify military detention and eviction from the civil justice system.

Movements of children's and adolescent rebellion like those of the Ultras have been crucial since 2007 to the development of a revolutionary way of life, as well as to the geography of resistance to policed, militarized, and media-corporate domination. Although not taken seriously or credited with developing an alternative ideology or political project for the revolution, Ultras present a bold and resilient form of unruly popular sovereignty. After the Port Said massacre, while the world focused on viewing Egypt through the imposed binary of the Brotherhood versus "liberals," the Ultras and other children's rebellions occupied streets and structures, and dominated the daily life of resistance in Cairo, Alexandria, and in the strategically critical Suez Canal cities for much of 2012 and 2013.

Egyptian Ultras have gradually emerged as narrative subjects of political and generational change, as well as objects of social and scholarly fascination. In 1993 the queer Egyptian filmmaker Yousry Nasrallah featured pro-Ultras soccer fan clubs in his popular film *Mercedes* (Holden 1995). The Ultras served as a kind of deus ex machina at the film's denouement, rescuing an artist from security-state thugs and redeeming the artist's gay brother who had been victimized by hypermasculine informants. In *Mercedes*, the Ultras smoothed generational and political divides and offered a playful, boisterous form of public pleasure that implied a possible embrace of tolerant humanist or populist celebration of sexuality in public. *Mercedes* gendered these Ultras as boyish but not as manly. They were represented and continue to represent themselves in contemporary street actions, in specific contrast to the steroidal hypermasculinity of the state-linked thugs and brutal police. This childish dimension of Ultra politics reflects not just transnational "soccer globalization" but also the particular Egyptian sociabilities of the children's sovereignties discussed above.

The Egyptian anthropologist Dalia Abdel Hamid (2014: 4–5) discusses the structural transformation and oligarchical corporate takeover in Egyptian sports that drove Ultras to come together as an activist community:

> Egypt in 2007, the year when those communities had been formed, was truly a neoliberal state. Everything was being privatized, education, health, transportation, and public-sector companies. Egypt was a perfect model for Harvey's story on neoliberalism, where the IMF and World Bank kept interfering in Egyptian economic decision[s], pushing for free trade and giving blind eye to the rising unemployment. [International Financial Institutions] prais[ed] the increase in national product and d[id]n't discuss its distribution. Football was not a different story in this respect. A small number of [the] bourgeois elite owned the clubs and profiteered from players' deals. On the other hand, the working class and students, the real spectators of the game, were banned from getting into these fancy clubs,

ha[d] no say in clubs' decisions and only permitted to be in the third grade section in the stadium.

In 2008 the Ultras began to turn against the state media, as well as against the police and corporate oligarchy, while the TV anchor Ahmed Shobeir stirred up queer panic and police violence against the Ultras. Abdel Hamid (2014: 6–7) writes:

> The famous sport TV anchor called Shobeir aired a very infamous video in 2008 in which members of Ultras Ahlawy AU07 are smoking hash and drinking alcohol and this incident coincided with mass arrest of Ultras members from their homes. Ever since, media outlets used to portray Ultras as deviants, drug addicts and homosexuals. . . . Escalated violence with police forces erupted in 2008 with the growing numbers of Ultras to be several thousands; police officers were terrorized by the organized fans. Ultras members started to defend themselves and respond to the police attack with counter attacks by throwing missiles into them and beat[ing] them up. There were several important incidents where Ultras managed to defeat security forces and make them run away. The most important one was just before the revolution by 10 days on the 15th of January 2011. It was a friendly match for Al-Ahly in Kafr El-Sheikh and police attacked the Ultras heavily when they celebrated the first goal. Ultras attacked them back and they managed to injure many police officers.

These confrontations came to a head after the ousting of President Mubarak, when the Supreme Council of the Armed Forces (SCAF) ruled as Egypt's transitional executive. On February 1, 2012, a brutal massacre took place in the main soccer stadium of Port Said. Armed forces vehicles surrounded the stadium, sealed off the exits, and Central Security (paramilitary police) forces blocked any fans from leaving. In the darkness and confusion, thugs among (or masquerading as) Ultras of the local Al-Masry club attacked the Ultras of the Cairo-based Ahlawy Club. In the horrifying melee that ensued, seventy young people were killed, chopped up by machetes or suffocated as they were blocked by the military at the exits. It was obvious to Ultras of both teams that this massacre had been planned and deployed by officials of the military and police as "punishment for their participation in the revolution. . . . The massacre was a turning point in the Ultras participation in the revolution" (Zirin 2012). As one of Abdel Hamid's respondents (2014: 7) reported, "The massacre crystallized the enmity between us and the SCAF. Now we organize marches and we had a sit-in and many protests.

Now we are present in all revolutionary activities and not only in confrontations and clashes."

Since the early 2000s, the Ultras have developed a unique fan culture and set of collective practices that set them at loggerheads with the apparatuses of the police state, as well as with the country's corporate elites. The Egyptian scholar Mohamed Elgohari (2013: 26–27) writes of Egypt's Ultras:

> The contention between the Ultras and the state/police is focused on a few key issues: First, the limits placed upon the Ultras freedom within the stadium created much tension between the state and the Ultras groups. Using the flames, fireworks, and pyrotechnics by the Ultras members in the stadiums was not allowed. In breaking that rule, the Ultras incited clashes between its members and the security forces, which generally resulted with the arrest of members of the Ultras. The Ultras sought to express themselves in support of their team within the stadium without any restriction or intervention from security officials. The Ultras always asserted the belief that the rules that govern the curva should be set by the fans themselves, not by oppressive police officers or by corrupted officials in the EFA. A second point of contention between the Ultras and the police revolved around freedom in creating graffiti. Liberating the public spaces and, more specifically, the public walls, from the political regime and state control was an important tool used by the Ultras.[5]

As Elgohari notes, street graffiti and murals that captured the dissident moral and parapolitical agenda of the Ultras became ubiquitous in urban Egypt and in the Canal Cities during this period. One style depicted boy martyrs, focusing on those killed in the Port Said massacre, but also depicting those killed in the battle between youth groups and the military—called the Battle of Mohammad Mahmoud Street—and those who died or were tortured to death in military detention or police custody. A second style repeated the text "Cops Are Whores," "Cops Are Fags," or "A.C.A.B." (All Cops Are Bastards), the latter being by far the most common. A third style depicted either Brotherhood leaders or military leaders as tricksters, liars, or snakes, embodying diabolical agendas. Often this style depicted leaders revealing their true identities as Satan, or as the Joker from the *Batman* franchise.

Each of these three representational styles resonates with queer dissidence, in a broad sense. Graffiti murals of boy martyrs add angel wings to the boys, who are depicted as smiling images of innocence and playfulness. These murals thus render boy martyrs definitely as children or cherubs, not as martyred soldiers or as valiant young men. Because of their beauty, murals or cherubic boy martyrs seem designed to stir the Ultras much-vaunted ethic of "love of fellow-fan," and "love of team," as much as to rally outrage. The third style of "trickster" graffiti also has some queer resonance: one mural depicts President Morsi as a rosy-cheeked queen of hearts, a false lady-luck played by the joker of the "deep state." The graffiti style that calls cops "fags" or "whores," combined with images of police partially dressed in women's clothing, or of police officers making out with each other, has been identified by some as homophobic. However, this style of graffiti could alternatively be read within the language of Ultras' intentionally vulgar chants, which mobilize intense attacks at the intersection of police repression, corporate sports and corporate media "star culture," and elitist oligarchical exclusion of "the people" from public space and sports. In the terminology of the Ultras, a "whore" or a "fag" or a "bastard" is someone, whether an athlete or fan, who sells out to the police to work as a provocateur or informant, or who sells out to work for corporate sports or the celebrity media.

In a climate in which the police, military, and media apparatus of the state were describing Ultras' "love of club and love of each other" as a culture of homosexuality, debauchery, vandalism, and (eventually) of "Black Bloc" terrorism, this style of seemingly homophobic graffiti can be read as an aggressive inversion of these queering terms. While police, media, and the military used these terms to smear the Ultras, Ultras used them as a critique of the oligarchical security state. Even certain young gay-identified Ultras and female former Ultras admitted to me that they relished the rowdy chants that labeled cops fags and whores, perhaps for this reason. The use of homophobic terms by Ultras against police can be seen as similar to other projects that reclaim terms used to target queer people, like the use of the derogatory term *queer* itself that has been reclaimed, since Ultras were being targeted and designated perverse by these terms.

These forms of junior queer dissidence and children's rebellion, which predate and persist beyond the logics of protest that occupied Tahrir Square in 2011, never came together as a specific "third way" or alternative political ideology or platform. However, these forms of expression and organization did and do embody what the Egyptian political scientist Ashraf El-Sherif (2012) calls a very serious "politics of fun." Though the security state, liberal civil society, and the moralistic leaders of the Islamist parties all agree that "stability" is top priority, the Ultras reject

> the paradigm of the depression, control, and normalization of apathy versus the paradigm of joyful liberation from the shackles of social and insti-

tutional norms to create gratifying chaos. . . . This conflict between two rhythms of life—one so dim it fails to realize its own fragility, stagnation and gradual extinction and the other so young and full of life that it fails to realize the revolutionary consequences of its actions—is a useful one. It should be allowed to grow. In fact, the chaos of the Ultras, Egypt's hardcore football fans, may play the role of waking up Egypt's middle class, which continues to adhere to the myth of stability. (Ibid.)

Conclusion

This essay has explored the highly sexualized and criminalized tensions between infantilization and humanization in the realm of militarized governance and security-state practices. Why is there such a failure to recognize children as agents when they swarm streets, protest sites, consumer hubs, and infrastructure facilities by the thousands in a constant eruption of challenges, claims, and expressions? I argue that we should not see these "children's" social formations as utopian figures of playfulness, indiscipline, or futurity (or failed futurity). Instead, scholars must ground these infantilized subjects, these children, in particular social geographies, political-economic structures of work, and political-traditions of unruly collective projection. My findings demonstrate the mechanisms and practices by which social actors branded as children challenge the regime of infantilization by launching alternative forms of collective work, street occupation, and expressive resignification.

On June 30, 2014, the prominent Middle East analyst Juan Cole (2014) argued:

> The young Arabs who made the recent revolutions are . . . distinctive: sub-stantially more urban, literate, media-savvy and wired than their parents and grandparents. . . . Analysts have tended to focus on the politics of the Arab youth revolutions and so have missed the more important, longer-term story of a generational shift in values, attitudes and mobilizing tactics. The youth movements were, in part, intended to provoke the holding of genuine, transparent elections, and yet the millennials were too young to stand for office when they happened.

Cole is known for taking a strong stand, insisting during dark times on reviving the hope identified with the "Facebook generation" slogans of 2011 and continu-ing to advocate a liberal futurism linked to the promise of youth as a force of modernity, democracy, and innovation. However, by June 2014, when he published this piece, this vision of the youth protester as tech-savvy futurist had been securitized—transformed or retransformed through figures of hypermasculinized Black Bloc anarchists or the ubiquitous discourse of "terrorism." Youth activists were facing severe repression by a revanchist security state in Egypt, near-extermination in Syria as they were squeezed between Islamic militias and Bashar al-Assad's state, and marginalization not just across the Middle East but also in Europe and the Americas, where a "revolutionary generation" had swept the global public sphere in 2010–12 in a way often compared to the "Generation of 1968."

What this discourse of youth as vehicles of liberal futurism missed, during its moment of triumph in 2011, as well as during attempts to revive it during the darker times of 2013–14, is the figure not of youth—university and graduate students in their twenties and thirties, young adult labor leaders, website managers and networkers—but of masses of children. These children—especially in the case of Egypt but also across many of the Arab Spring countries—mobilized by the thousands, pushing state and political discourse in radically different directions from those of their "big brothers and sisters" in the youth movements. Children are particularly important political actors and subjects of security and morality politics because they reveal queer aspects of the logics of Arab revolution and global counterrevolution in a way that the ubiquitous focus on youth ignores. At the intersection of securitizing and infantilizing politics is the figure of the loose child, the child on the loose, overwhelming borders and security perimeters. Critical, situated, contextualized forms of research and sociopolitical bridge building need to wholly rethink, and recognize in new ways, the spongy and disruptive subject of the child, the categories that have been erected to infantilize politics and violently operate on them, and the queer logics of unruly dissent that play out when those security apparatuses are interrupted.

Those labeled children once they enter, unleashed, into the realm of public protest or the street occupations are queered, marked by the security state and humanitarian apparatuses as dangerously precocious, trafficking in their own *inhiraf* sexuality. Or, these children are reidentified as exploited minors instrumentalized by nefarious adults to pervert and undermine the home, the nation, the economy, or worse, to disrupt the normal boundaries between these spaces, imposing their *'efreet* sovereignty. But "children" have every prerogative to take a stand on this contemporary global regime of infantilization, in the broadest spaces and scales. And they do take stands. Collective actions of "children" can turn this queering logic inside out, repacing flows and commutes, swarming and overloading circuits of child labor. The ingenuity, expressiveness, and work of children's agency—including its violence and sexuality—merit recognition in their own global and local histories, political economies and symbolic geographies.

Notes

I am deeply grateful for the hard work, inspiration, patience, and sheer brilliance offered by this special issue's editors, Julian Gill-Peterson, Rebekah Sheldon, and Kathryn Bond Stockton, as well as by the illumination and tirelessness of *GLQ* editors Beth Freeman and Jessica Neasbitt. I would also like to thank the peer reviewers for their in-depth engagement with this work. And I would like to convey my gratitude to the scholars and communities at Indiana University, University of Massachusetts Amherst, American University in Beirut, USC, the International Feminist Politics Conference, the Brazilian Political Science Association Conference, and the Arab Studies Association General Assembly, where I presented various drafts of this study and received crucial input and generous support. I am grateful for research funding for this project provided by the Arab Council of the Social Sciences and the Academic Senate of the University of California, Santa Barbara.

1. Use of the term *surge* to describe this collective agency of migrant children traveling without parents sounded the loudest of alarms, as it resonated with military-humanitarian connotations of counterinsurgency surges in wartime and evoked disaster and emergency coverage of looming superstorms or hurricanes (Munro 2014; Human Rights Watch 2014).
2. I put the term *children* in quotes here to underline what I see as the constructed character of infantilization that inscribes children as either subjects of developmentalism or play, not of politics.
3. These boots on the head reference a famous quotation from *1984*: "If you want a vision of the future, imagine a boot stamping on a human face—for ever" (Orwell 1949: 46).
4. I analyzed these new security agents in my book *The Security Archipelago* in terms of what I called the "baltagi effect" and the security state's confrontation with subjects of radical gendered resistance (see Amar 2013).
5. Originally from Italian, but now part of global Ultras terminology, *curva* means the curved seats behind the goal where the most fanatic supporters cluster.

References

AbdelAzim, Maha. 2014. "AFP Photo Depicts 'Child Endangerment': Human Rights Lawyer." *Daily News Egypt*, January 28. dailynewsegypt.com/2014/01/28/afp -photo-depicts-child-endangerment-human-rights-lawyer/.

Abdel Hamid, Dalia. 2014. "Ultras, State, and Revolution in Egypt." Master's thesis (in progress), American University, Cairo.

Ahram Online. 2014. "Updated: Article Proposing Idea of Killing Egyptian Street Children Stirs Fury." June 29. english.ahram.org.eg/NewsContent/1/64/104271/Egypt /Politics-/Article-proposing-idea-of-killing-Egyptian-street-.aspx.

Al Arabiya News. 2013. "Women Group Accuses Egypt's Brotherhood of Using Children at Sit-ins." August 3. english.alarabiya.net/en/News/middle-east/2013/08/03/Women -group-accuses-Egypt-s-Brotherhood-of-using-children-at-sit-ins.html.

Albawaba. 2011. "Child Labor in Egypt on the Rise." July 18. www.albawaba.com/main -headlines/child-labor-egypt-rise-383588.

Ali, Nelly. 2011. "The Vulnerability and Resilience of Street Children." *Global Studies of Childhood* 1, no. 3: 260–64. doi:10.2304/gsch.2011.1.3.260.

Amar, Paul. 2013. *The Security Archipelago: Human-Security States, Sexuality Politics, and the End of Neoliberalism.* Durham, NC: Duke University Press.

Ambrust, Walter. 2002. "The Riddle of Ramadan: Media, Consumer Culture, and the "Christianization" of a Muslim Holiday." In *Everyday Life in the Muslim Middle East*, 2nd ed., edited by Donna Lee Bowen and Evelyn A. Early, 335–48. Bloomington: Indiana University Press.

Aptekar, Lewis. 1988. *Street Children of Cali.* Durham, NC: Duke University Press.

———. 1989. "Characteristics of the Street Children of Colombia." *Child Abuse and Neglect: The International Journal* 13, no. 3: 427–39.

Ariès, Philippe. 1962. *Centuries of Childhood: A Social History of Family Life.* Translated by Robert Baldick. New York: Vintage.

Associated Press. 2005. "Spongebob, Muppets, Sister Sledge Writer Suffer Criticism." *USA Today*, January 22. usatoday30.usatoday.com/life/television/2005-01-22-kids -video_x.htm.

Bakhtin, Mikhail. 1984. *Rabelais and His World.* Bloomington: Indiana University Press.

BBC News. 2005. "US Right Attacks SpongeBob Video." January 20. news.bbc.co.uk/2 /hi/world/Americas/4190699.stm.

Beach, Alastair. 2013. "Egypt's Child Abuse Scourge." *Daily Beast*, February 22. www .thedailybeast.com/articles/2013/02/22/the-scourge-of-child-abuse-in-egypt-s -prisons.html.

Berger, Miriam. 2013. "SpongeBob SquarePants Takes Over Egypt." *BuzzFeed World*, October 23. www.buzzfeed.com/miriamberger/spongebob-sqaurepants-takes -over-egypt.

Bernstein, Robin. 2011. *Racial Innocence: Performing American Childhood and Race from Slavery to Civil Rights.* New York: New York University Press.

Bibars, Iman. 1998. "Street Children in Egypt: From the Home to the Street to Inappropriate Corrective Institutions." *Environment and Urbanization* 10, no. 1: 201–16. eau.sagepub.com/content/10/1/201.full.pdf.

Chouiten, Lynda. 2012. "A Carnivalesque Mirage: The Orient in Isabelle Eberhardt's

Writings." PhD diss., NUI Galway University. aran.library.nuigalway.ie/handle /10379/3600.

Cole, Juan. 2014. "Why It's Way Too Soon to Give Up on the Arab Spring." *Los Angeles Times*, June 28. www.latimes.com/opinion/op-ed/la-oe-cole-arab-spring-millenials -20140629-story.html.

Crain, Patricia. 1999. "Childhood as Spectacle." *American Literary History* 11: 545–53.

Edelman, Lee. 2004. *No Future: Queer Theory and the Death Drive.* Durham, NC: Duke University Press.

El Feky, Amira. 2013. "Street Children: What They Are Not." *Daily News Egypt*, April 14. www.dailynewsegypt.com/2013/04/14/street-children-what-they-are-not/.

Elgohari, Mohamed. 2013. "The Ultras Political Role and the State in Egypt." MA thesis, New York University. fordifp.net/Portals/0/Thesis/0b5156c0-783e-4fbe-a3e7 -032f1872e9daThe%20Ultras%20Political%20Role%20and%20the%20State %20in%20Egypt.pdf.

El Shakry, Omnia. 1998. "Schooled Mothers and Structured Play." In *Remaking Women: Feminism and Modernity in the Middle East*, edited by Lila Abu-Lughod, 126–70. Princeton: Princeton University Press.

———. 2007. *The Great Social Laboratory: Subjects of Knowledge in Colonial and Post-colonial Egypt.* Stanford: Stanford University Press.

———. 2011. "Youth as Peril and Promise: The Emergency of Adolescent Psychology in Postwar Egypt." *International Journal of Middle East Studies* 43, no. 4: 591–610.

El-Sherif, Ashraf. 2012. "The Ultras' Politics of Fun Confront Tyranny. *Jadaliyya*, February 5. www.jadaliyya.com/pages/index/4243/the-ultras-politics-of-fun -confront-tyranny-.

Enloe, Cynthia. 1990. "Womenandchildren: Making Feminist Sense of the Persian Gulf Crisis." *Village Voice*, September 25.

Fahmi, Kamal. 2007. *Beyond the Victim: The Politics and Ethics of Empowering Cairo's Street Children.* Cairo: American University in Cairo Press.

Farrag, Ola. 2013. "FACE for Children in Need: Building a Sustainable Street Children Youth Project in Cairo, Egypt." FACE Annual 2013 Report. facechildren.org/upload /files/FACE%20for%20Children%20in%20Need%20-%20Salam%20Street%20 Children%20Program%20Annual%20Report%202013.pdf.

Feteha, Ahmed. 2011. "1.6 Million Underage Workers in Egypt: Official Figures." *Ahram Online*, July 14. english.ahram.org.eg/NewsContent/3/12/16406/Business/Economy /-million-underage-workers-in-Egypt-Official-figure.aspx.

Frykberg, Mel. 2015. "Children of the Palestinian Revolution." DW Online, July 22. www.dw.com/en/children-of-the-palestinian-revolution/a-18596912.

Halberstam, J. Jack. 2011. *The Queer Art of Failure.* Durham, NC: Duke University Press.

Halberstam, Jack. 2013. "The Wild: Humans, Animals, Anarchy." Paper presented at
the Core Management Center of the Birkbeck Institute for Social Research, London,
December 10.

Hasso, Frances. 2010. *Consuming Desires: Family Crisis and the State in the Middle East.*
Durham, NC: Duke University Press.

Holden, Stephen. 1995. *"Mercedes* (1993) Film Review." *New York Times,* May 5. www
.nytimes.com/movie/review?res=990CE7D71438F936A35756C0A963958260.

Human Rights Watch. 2003a. "Charged with Being Children: Egyptian Police Abuse
of Children in Need of Protection." February 18. www.hrw.org/report/2003/02/18
/charged-being-children/egyptian-police-abuse-children-need-protection.

———. 2003b. "Mass Arrests of Street Children in Egypt." February 19. www.hrw.org
/news/2003/02/19/mass-arrests-street-children-egypt.

Human Rights Watch. 2014. "US: Surge in Detention of Child Migrants." June 25. www
.hrw.org/news/2014/06/25/us-surge-detention-child-migrants.

Hussein, N. H. 2003. *Street Children in Egypt: Group Dynamics and Subcultural Constitu-
ents.* Cairo Papers in Social Science, no. 2. Cairo: American University in Cairo Press.

International Labor Organization (ILO) and Egyptian Central Agency for Public Mobilization and Statistics (CAPMAS). 2012. *Working Children in Egypt: Results of the 2010
National Child Labor Survey.* Cairo: ILO.

International Organization for Migration (IOM) Cairo. 2011. "Street Children in Egypt:
Key Findings of a Study Conducted by the National Center for Social and Criminal
Change." Infographic. egypt.iom.int/Doc/Street%20children%20profile.pdf.

Katz, Cindi. 2008. "Childhood as Spectacle: Relays of Anxiety and the Reconfiguration of
the Child." *Cultural Geographies* 15, no. 1: 15–17. doi:10.177/1474474007085773.

Kingsley, Patrick. 2013. "How SpongeBob Became Massive in Egypt." *Guardian,* May 27.
www.theguardian.com/world/shortcuts/2013/may/27/spongebob-squarepants-egypt
-cartoon-fame.

Lippincott, Jacob. 2013. "Dispatch from Cairo: The Pyramid Scheme of Violence-Ravaged
Egypt." *Week,* March 12. theweek.com/article/index/241162/dispatch-from-cairo-the
-pyramid-scheme-of-violence-ravaged-egypt.

Masr, Mada. 2014. "Mother Defends Daughter Accused of Exploiting Street Children."
Morning Digest, May 6. www.madamasr.com/content/mother-defends-daughter
-accused-exploiting-street-children.

Mazidi, Amr. 2014. "Bi-l-ṣuwar: Shabaka tajnīd al-aṭfāl li-l-mushāraka bi-l-mudhāhirāt
tataza"amuhā amrīkīya" ("Photos: Arrest of Network Recruiting Children for Participation in US-Led Demonstrations") (the double ' ' is double ع), *al-Dastur,* May 4.
www.dostor.org/411903.

Mikdashi, Maya. 2014. "Can Palestinian Men Be Victims?" Jadaliyya.com, July 23.
www.jadaliyya.com/pages/index/18644/can-palestinian-men-be-victims
-gendering-israels-w.

Muñoz, José Esteban. 2012. "The Brown Commons: The Sense of Wildness." Paper presented at the Harry Ransom Humanities Research Center, University of Texas, Austin, October 12.

Munro, Neil. 2014. "Surge of Migrant Children Urged on by US-Based Parents." *Daily Caller*, July 14. dailycaller.com/2014/07/14/surge-of-migrant-children-urged-on-by -us-based-parents/.

Nader, Aya. 2016. "Couple Spend Their Wedding Money on Street Children, Wind Up in Egyptian Prison." *Egyptian Streets*, February 12. egyptianstreets.com/2016/02/12 /couple-spend-their-wedding-money-on-street-children-end-up-in-an-egyptian -prison/.

Nelson, Soraya Sarhaddi. 2012. "Egypt's Street Kids Are Revolution's Smallest Soldiers." *All Things Considered*, January 4. www.npr.org/2012/01/04/144692425/egypts -street-kids-are-revolutions-smallest-soldiers.

Orwell, George. 1949. *1984*. New York: Harcourt, Brace. msxnet.org/orwell/1984.

Park, Haeyoun. 2014. "Children at the Border." *New York Times*, October 21. www .nytimes.com/interactive/2014/07/15/us/questions-about-the-border-kids.html ?_r=0.

Patel, Sheela. 1990. "Street Children, Hotel Boys, and Children of Pavement Dwellers and Construction Workers in Bombay: How They Meet Their Daily Needs." *Environment and Urbanization* 2, no. 2: 9–26. eau.sagepub.com/content/2/2/9.abstract.

Petersen, Mark Allen. 2013. "In SpongeBob We Trust?" *Connected in Cairo*, November 2. connectedincairo.com/2013/11/02/in-spongebob-we-trust.

Pinho, Osmundo. 2014. "Black Bodies, Wrong Places: Spatial and Morality Politics of Rolezinho Racialized Youth 'Invasions' and Police Repression in the Public Spaces of Today's Brazil." Lecture, Interdisciplinary Humanities Center, University of California, Santa Barbara, March 3.

Pursley, Sara. 2013. "The Stage of Adolescence: Anticolonial Time, Youth Insurgency, and the Marriage Crisis in Hashimite Iraq." *History of the Present* 3, no. 2: 160–97. doi10.5406/historypresent.3.2.0160.

Schielke, Samuli. 2015. *Egypt in the Future Tense: Hope, Frustration, and Ambivalence before and after 2011*. Bloomington: Indiana University Press.

Schielke, Samuli, and Jessica Winegar. 2012. "The Writing on the Walls of Egypt." *Middle East Research and Information Project (MER)* 265. www.merip.org/mer/mer265 /writing-walls-egypt.

Shorter, Edward. 1975. *The Making of the Modern Family*. New York: Basic Books.

Stockton, Kathryn Bond. 2009. *The Queer Child, or Growing Sideways in the Twentieth Century*. Durham, NC: Duke University Press.

Stockton, Kathryn Bond. 2016. "The Queer Child Now and Its Paradoxical Global Effects." *GLQ* 22, no. 4: 505–40.

Sweiss, Rania Kassab. 2012. "Saving Egypt's Village Girls: Humanity, Rights, and Gendered Vulnerability in a Global Youth Initiative." *Journal of Middle East Women's Studies* 8, no. 2: 26–50.

UNICEF Egypt. 2000. "Street Children: Issues and Impact." www.unicef.org/egypt /protection_4397.html.

———. 2004. "Primary School Years." www.unicef.org/egypt/children_152.html.

Winegar, Jessica, and Lara Deeb, eds. 2015. *Anthropology's Politics: Disciplining the Middle East*. Stanford: Stanford University Press.

Zaretsky, Eli. 1976. *Capitalism, the Family, and Personal Life*. New York: Harper and Row.

Zirin, Dave. 2012. "The Ultras and the Revolution." socialistworker.org/2012/02/13/the -ultras-and-the-revolution.

SEXUAL ORPHANINGS

Mary Zaborskis

Native Queer Childhood

*T*his essay is about orphans and orphaning, queerness and queering. An orphan is a child without parents, a child who has either been permanently abandoned or whose parents are dead; in the United States, an orphan is also a ward of the state. I argue that the process through which Native American children were taken from reservations and required to attend boarding schools in the nineteenth and twentieth centuries is usefully understood as a state-produced orphaning, an orphaning away from Indian customs and culture and ultimately toward death. The education that children received in boarding schools can be seen as a process of further, mandatory orphaning, one that children learned to enact on themselves. The intensity with which these boarding schools intervened in the sexuality of Native children was crucial to this process, and I argue that "sexual orphaning" was the goal of the boarding schools' alienation of Native children from their culture, a goal that queered children away from futurity and away from reproductivity. This queering was achieved paradoxically through heterosexualization, but a racialized heterosexualization oriented toward failure—they would never be straight (or white) in the settler state's eyes. The ultimate goal of my argument is to suggest that the familiar coupling of "queer" with "no future" proposed by Lee Edelman (2004) is especially distressing for Native studies, and I conclude by asking, instead, what "erotics" might remain for these orphans and look at how the genocidal sexual orphanings of Native children might be recalibrated in Native fiction toward survivance rather than disappearance.

This essay takes up a particular version of racialized and sexualized childhood: Native American queer childhood. In Kathryn Bond Stockton's *The Queer Child, or Growing Sideways in the Twentieth Century*, one version of the queer child she proposes is the *child queered by color*, or the racialized queer child. While children are often synonymous with innocence, the child queered by color is

GLQ 22:4
DOI 10.1215/10642684-3603114
© 2016 by Duke University Press

incapable of that innocence.[1] The innocent child is free of a past, which is understood as "antithetical to childhood" (Stockton 2009: 30), even though the child's
very innocence is the product of adults' desire for a "preferred past" (Bruhm and
Hurley 2004: xiii). Adults narrate some children as blank slates not because they
are but because adults want them to be.

Racialized queer children, however, are queered by a historical past, and
in the case of Native children, by a settler-narrated past. In other words, Native
children are incapable of innocence because of settler ideology that has viewed
Natives as backward, deviant, and dangerous—that is, queer. By "queer," I mean
that the state and its institutions and agents structure gender, sexuality, and kinship for children so that settler understandings and practices are "straight," and
anything Native is consequently not-straight and thus queer.[2] This definition of
queerness is drawn from Mark Rifkin's scholarship in *When Did Indians Become
Straight?*, in which Rifkin (2011: 5–6) explores how "coordinated assault on native
social formations . . . [can] be understood as an organized effort to make heterosexuality compulsory as a key part of breaking up indigenous landholdings." The
settler state intervened into and violently restructured—or straightened—Native
traditions, customs, and kinship to justify violent dispossession of Native land.
The parenting nation narrates queerness in an effort to normalize, naturalize, and
instantiate heteronormativity, which enables settler claims on land, property, and
inheritance. Adult or child, all Natives have been and continue to be queered by
this narrative. Native children in particular have been crucial to the settler state's
attempts to queer Native communities. Since the turn of the century, this queering has served to justify and enable state-sanctioned genocide under the guise of
welfare and false promises of protection—the future functions as a trap, enabling
violence. Innocent children, seen as free of a past, can enter the future; racialized
queer children, seen as having a past, are barred from the future, and this barring
is enacted precisely through promising futurity.

The boarding school system of the late nineteenth and twentieth centuries
in the United States and Canada was the mechanism through which many Native
children were made to experience queer childhood. Producing queer childhood
was pivotal for eliminating indigenous populations through proclaimed assimilation of their children. Children were removed from their reservations and required
to attend the boarding schools, where they were violently forced to abandon their
names, languages, and cultural practices. At school, they were educated to look
back and understand their Native communities and culture as queer and something to abandon, an education that occurred alongside all-but-institutionalized
sexual abuse.

I understand this abandonment as an orphaning and see it as a mandate for those Native children who passed through the boarding school. The boarding schools produced Native children as orphans in order to enforce metaphorical orphanings of Indianness. By Indianness, I mean all those features whose loss would facilitate cultural genocide—languages, custom, and practices and understandings of kinship, gender, and sexuality. I term the state-enforced abandonment of the latter a *sexual orphaning*, and its metaphorical loss had material effects: orphaning children from Native conceptualizations of gender and sexuality alienated children from Native acculturated bodies, and this alienation oriented children toward nonreproductivity. I conceptualize sexual orphaning as a historical process that produced bodily practices, sensations, and affects lived out in the bodies of targeted children. Drawing on Rifkin's scholarship in *Erotics of Sovereignty* (2012), I understand these practices and sensations as "erotics—sensations of pleasure, desire, memory, wounding, and interrelation with others, the land, and ancestors" (39). Queering Native children necessitated an education in erotics: how to apprehend them and how to disavow them. The schools educated children to understand and experience erotics as shameful, but these shamed erotics created avenues for decolonization. In her reading of M. Jacqui Alexander's concept of "radical self-possession," Ann Cvetkovich (2012: 25) explains how decolonization can and must include "the senses and feelings." Building on this claim, I argue that the Native child's body, a strategic target of colonization carried out by the boarding school and its agents, has a capacity for decolonization at the level of the individual body by reclaiming those senses and pleasures that education forces the child to disavow.

Sexual orphanings are a key feature of Native queer childhood: they both queer Native children and compel these children to orphan their sexuality. The attempt to orphan children from their sexuality was twofold. First, schools imposed heteronormative understandings of gender and sexuality on children, and this imposition necessitated that children renounce Native understandings of gender and sexuality, viewing them now as backward and sinful (Rifkin 2011; Morgensen 2010). Second, school agents violated children's bodies through sexual abuse that was "indeed institutionalized as to almost form a core part of the curriculum" (Schneider 2010: 18). Chris Finley (2011: 32) argues that "for many tribes . . . shame around sex started in the boarding schools, and sexual shame has been passed down for generations." Sexual orphanings did not make all children nonreproductive—there are generations who still bear the legacy of those who survived the school, who are also testament to the ongoing presence of Native peoples and sexuality in the face of attempts at erasure. However, Finley suggests a pervasive shame whose origin is in the schools, one that haunts many indigenous communities and has affected how Natives view and experience sexuality: it is filtered through a history of abuse.

Abuse and education in the schools helped the settler state center its understandings of sexuality. This sexuality, which Scott Morgensen (2010: 106) calls "settler sexuality," permits a narrow heteronormativity for white bodies while sanctioning sexual violence against and abuse of nonwhite bodies. Settler sexuality casts as queer more capacious understandings of sexuality that consider dispositions, affect, pleasure, and sensations, or what Rifkin terms *erotics*. Sexual orphanings make it difficult to inhabit erotics because of alienation from the Native acculturated body. Rifkin (2012: 28) alludes to how more capacious understandings of sexuality are especially important for considering Native resistance because "sexuality points to a nexus of practices, desires, relations, and pleasures in which one could locate the presence of modes of indigeneity that exceed the 'oppressed, repressed, shamed, and *imposed* sense of reality' generated through institutionalized processes of settlement." In other words, the settler state and its institutions—such as the boarding school—enforce an "*imposed* sense of reality" onto Native sexuality that narrate it as a source of shame and oppression. Here, Rifkin invites us to think about what to do with the presences of "desires" and "pleasures" that exist within and despite seemingly totalizing narratives of "oppress[ion]," "repress[ion]," and "shame."

I use this invitation to return to Native queer childhood as produced by and experienced in the boarding school. Sexual damage is a hallmark of the settler education of Native children. The violence, abuse, and neglect in schools that the settler state allowed to continue for close to a century is undeniable and inexcusable. I want to focus, however, on some unexpected effects of sexual damage. Accounts of Native queer childhood in the boarding school force us to contend with the presence of desire and pleasure amid violence and abuse, as well as the alternative times and spaces they might open up. How does pleasure come about in this setting? What do these moments of pleasure unsettle? How might they disrupt totalizing narratives of the school's production of oppression and shame? How much weight does pleasure actually carry in the context of ongoing genocide? Does pleasure enable access to alternative times and spaces, and if so, how? An examination of Native queer childhood asks us to consider the knotted problem of violence's relation to decolonization. Children are an optic for apprehending and disrupting settler narratives of unmitigated colonization and disappearance; the schools and their agents colonize children's bodies, but this colonization did not go uncontested by children.

The unique historical processes surrounding the queering of nineteenth- and twentieth-century Native children invite us to more fully explore this form of sexualized and racialized childhood. Scholars have worked on racialized and queer childhood but have not paid sustained attention to queer children in an indigenous context. I examine the historical production of these children, and, in order to consider the questions and problems surrounding an investigation of Native queer childhood, I turn to *Kiss of the Fur Queen* (1998), by the Cree author and playwright Tomson Highway, whose fictional text imagines possibilities for survival and indigeneity *despite* the historical phenomenon of sexual orphanings. Highway's novel functions as a counterarchive, recounting the sexual orphanings two brothers are forced to undergo, but also exploring how children might maintain a connection to their sexuality, even in the context of violent education and abuse.

The boarding school is a nineteenth- and twentieth-century historical institution whose effects are ongoing; looking at a contemporary text that represents the boarding school is important to the present because Native children, most visibly in the modern-day foster care system, continue to be targets of settler policy that seeks to erase indigenous presence under the guise of welfare, putting children in often precarious situations. The only future for Native children is the white future they help preserve; Bethany Schneider (2015: 87) contends that "Native children are the diet of white supremacy and colonization," enabling settler futures not intended for them. The boarding schools educated children in a normativity to which they could never accede, guaranteeing the failure of the Native body: children are unable to grow up or move forward into a reproductive future. They are left, as Stockton (2009: 6) puts it, to "grow sideways," and I grapple with the pleasures and possibilities accessible to children in this liminal space to which the schools orient them. I examine the history of the boarding schools, which helps us understand how sexual orphanings that position children for no future exist in a larger context that neglects the Native body through biopolitical practices. I then turn to *Kiss of the Fur Queen* as a text to think through the issues of violence, pleasure, and decolonization in Native queer childhood, considering how sexual orphanings are enforced in the narrative and looking at alternative modes of embodiment that Highway imagines as possible responses to an education that leaves children orphaned from their bodies and sexualities.

Managing Children at the Boarding School

While I focus on literal children in my essay, it is important to understand how the settler state has historically narrated Native Americans as figural children to justify colonization and deny Native communities sovereignty. In *Fathers and Children*, Michael Rogin ([1975] 2008: 11) examines the rhetoric and actions of US president Andrew Jackson, engineer of the 1830 Indian Removal Act, to reveal how his carefully manufactured project of "'inevitable' Indian extinction" necessitated a conceptual kinship reordering. Jackson and his contemporaries conceived of Natives as stuck in the time of "'childhood' of the human race," whereas white males were understood to be endowed with an "adult white maturity" (ibid.: 6, 8), which legitimized their role as the rule-wielding parent nation. The settler state's perceived duty to discipline indigenous populations materialized in policy that sanctioned genocide and legalized the seizure of Native land. Through these acts, the father nation "grounded their growing up in a securely achieved manhood, and securely possessed [Native] land" (ibid.: 125).

Kinship rhetoric continued to be deployed to explain why Native communities needed to be under the settler state's parental care. In the introduction to "Sexuality, Nationality, Indigeneity," a special issue of *GLQ*, Schneider (2010: 17) points us to a critical statement in Chief Justice John Marshall's decision in the 1831 *Cherokee Nation v. Georgia* case, where he suggested that Native Nations' relationship to the United States "resembles that of a ward to a guardian." Schneider's (2010: 20) reading of this seminal definition of Native nations understands the dynamic of father nation / colonized child as one where "Native people . . . were requeered as children, eternally stunted, the sexualized wards of the state." This maneuver was a "requeer[ing]," since the state initially "queered" Native culture and sexuality by casting it as deviant and backward; the "sexual[ization]" of Natives was a heterosexualization, as the state attempted to "force Indians into a heteronormative futurity defined by private property, inheritance, and the nuclear family" (ibid.). For the United States to gain access to the land, it made Native people into "wards of the state," orphaned communities who must be taken care of by the parenting nation.[3]

A crucial step in creating orphaned communities was intervening in, destroying, and restructuring kinship structures to fit into colonial understandings of personhood and property relations. Rifkin (2011: 8) has demonstrated how "imperial interventions into Native residency, family formation, collective decision-making, resource distribution, and land tenure" broke down Native traditions, customs, and kinship formation to achieve this violent restructuring. And, to make sure that many of these interventions would succeed, the state targeted children, most visibly in the form of educational policies focused on assimilation.

The first off-reservation Indian boarding school that produced queer Native orphans in the United States was the Carlisle Indian Industrial School. Founded by Colonel Richard Henry Pratt in 1879 and in operation until 1918, the school served as a model for other Indian boarding schools that proliferated in the latter half of the twentieth century in the United States and Canada. These institutions that emerged out of child removal policies functioned as biopolitical tools of the settler state because they helped control indigenous kinship and futurity. Michel Foucault ([1976] 2003: 245) explains that "biopolitics deals with the population, with the population as [a] political problem, as a problem that is at once scientific and political, as a biological problem and as power's problem." The "population" of indigenous peoples had to be managed, and management of children functioned as a ruse for furthering the mission to eliminate Natives from the colonial landscape. The settler state's intervention into kinship was an intervention into indigenous reproduction, and children helped the settler state exercise its "power to 'make' live and 'let' die" (ibid.: 241). As Margaret Jacobs (2009: 4) explains, "Indigenous child removal constituted another crucial way to eliminate indigenous people, both in a cultural and a biological sense"—the children were stripped of their Indianness in the schools; forced to abandon their languages, cultural practices, names; and separated for years if not a lifetime from their indigenous communities, accounting for the cultural elimination that Jacobs describes.

While biological elimination of indigenous tribes started with the arrival of the first settlers in North America, the turn of the twentieth century marks a shift from biological elimination through war to cultural elimination through assimilation. However, the latter did not preclude the former. Patrick Wolfe (2006: 398–99) asserts that "the imposition on a people of the procedures and techniques that are generally glossed as 'cultural genocide' is certainly going to have a direct impact on that people's capacity to stay alive." In other words, trying to rid children of their Indianness culturally has a "direct impact" on their chances for survival. Sexual orphanings, a consequence of cultural genocidal tactics, enabled cultural genocide to effect biological elimination under the guise of welfare.

One immediate way schools affected Native futurity was by neglecting students' health, resulting in many deaths. A brief look at the conditions of the schools shows that they were sites where children's "capacity to stay alive" was compromised. From their inaugural moment in 1879, boarding schools operated as institutions that took in healthy children and made them unhealthy. Lack of regulation and oversight made it so that schools were never an environment that fostered health, growth, and general well-being. Schools produced what Jasbir Puar (2011: 153) terms "debilitated bodies," and this created debility, exacerbated by disregard for the limits on children's capacity for manual labor, hastened the "slow death" (Berlant 2011: 95) of Native populations. Debility meant that fewer children had to be educated and the state desire for the "Vanishing Indian" was fulfilled, allowing the state to expend fewer resources on fewer Indians. In his report on the comprehensive state of Indian health, the physician Everett Rhoades (1976: 28) explains that at the end of the nineteenth century, "when the federal Government assumed responsibility for the education of Indians, some degree of responsibility for their health was incidentally involved, and the first expenditures for their health was made from funds appropriated for education and 'civilization.'" In other words, concern for Indian children's health was "incidental," and there were no funds specifically allocated to oversee health and regulate living conditions in Indian boarding schools. As a result, many children never saw a physician, and they were not examined for preexisting illnesses or symptoms prior to enrolling in the schools.

Sequestered in this restrictive environment that was supposedly committed to civilizing its wards, children were forced to live in squalid conditions. Many became ill when arriving at the schools because of environmental factors. Children sent east experienced harsh climatic changes, not to mention the physiological stress of travel itself, but they did not receive any medical attention once they arrived. For example, David DeJong (2008) shares how a group of fifteen Shoshone boys were sent to Carlisle, and eleven died shortly after arrival. Children experienced overcrowding, often sleeping two or three to a bed in closed quarters that had poor ventilation. The food available at schools resulted in inadequate nutrition, which was especially concerning because children were forced to engage in strenuous physical labor. These conditions, coupled with "strict military discipline," meant "some schools . . . became synonymous with death and disease" (DeJong 2007: 261–62). DeJong (2007) outlines how illnesses, including tuberculosis, smallpox, and trachoma, were widespread in schools at levels statistically more significant than among white people. Furthermore, when children became fatally ill, they were often sent back to their reservations; this practice allowed infected children to come in contact with their uninfected communities, enabling the transit and transmission of illness among Natives. Racist ideology fueled in part by social Darwinism considered Indian children, even if civilized, nonwhite and thus inferior and justified to be less invested in than their white counterparts (ibid.: 274–75). The state's oversight of its own institutions worked to "'let' die" Native children.

For those who did pass through and survive the boarding school, the schools sought to educate them in ways that would ensure no future for Natives. The often-cited motto of the schools, "Kill the Indian, save the man" (Pratt [1908] 1979: 46), captures the schools' violent project of ridding children of their Indianness to "save" their humanity—for their Indianness was conceived as nonhuman.

This motto exemplifies Russ Castronovo's (2001) theory of necro citizenship, or the ways that the state necessitates a death, especially for members of marginalized groups, before an individual can be made into a political subject. This necessary "death that structures national identity" (ibid.: 6) *is* the orphaning that children must undergo. Orphaning Indianness is synonymous with "kill[ing] the Indian"—the projects are one and the same, inextricably linked because educating children to orphan their Indianness enables the state to eliminate Indians. If children abandon their Indianness, they cannot sustain Native lineages; Native reproductivity stalls, and Natives start to disappear from the colonial landscape. The settler state's attempt to orphan the Native child functions to ensure no future for indigenous peoples as well as indigenous modes of being.

Pratt's rhetoric positioned Indian children as the means through which a future would be secured for both themselves and their tribes. In his treatise on the development of the schools, Pratt ([1908] 1979: 20) writes about how he convinced the Sioux to send their children away: "Your own welfare while you live and the welfare of your children after you, and all your interests in every way, demand that your children should have the same education that the white man has." But this "same education" did not mean the same future as settlers; according to Pratt, Indian children could be "convert[ed] in all ways but color" (ibid.: 5) and thus could never fully enter into white civilization. Rifkin (2011: 150) reiterates this point, explaining that eventual "interracial coupling" with whites was never foreseen for these children; the schools vehemently "preserv[ed] the reproductively constituted color line while arguing for a malleability in Indian character." In other words, the Native body would never permit children to take part in a white future, regardless of how much the state altered their "Indian character." Thus, the children were educated to abandon Indianness culturally, but they would never be able to leave behind their Native bodies in the eyes of the state; politically, legally, socially, and biologically, they could never be white citizens. But without their heritage or an understanding of Native customs, traditions, or languages, their Native bodies could not reproduce Indianness. "Kill the Indian, save the man" could succeed—except that "the man" saved was the white community that the state never intended for the children to join.[4] In other words, "Kill the Indian, save the man" is a peculiar kind of orphaning; the inability of orphaned children to carry on Indianness through the Native body preserves the future for white bodies at the expense of a generation of orphaned Native children, suspended in a liminal space between whiteness and Indianness, past and future. Children's bodies are the vestiges of this orphaning; since the body remains, the schools needed to alienate children from these bodies to succeed in a complete orphaning of Indianness.

The state, then, attempted to complete this orphaning from the body through queering Native childhood, and crucially through the sexual orphanings that enabled this queer production. Children were paradoxically queered through being educated in white heterosexual norms. This queering was a double bind. On the one hand, the boarding schools' ostensible heterosexualization of Native children orphaned them from indigenous modes of sexuality; on the other hand, that heterosexualization was racialized so as to arrive at normative failure, leaving Native children in a liminal space.

Sexual Orphanings in *Kiss of the Fur Queen*

I now turn to Highway's *Kiss of the Fur Queen* to explore how sexual orphanings are enforced and consider what possibilities the text imagines despite these orphanings—can they be disrupted? Undone? Reversed? Paying attention to the bodily sensations that the orphanings effect in *Kiss of the Fur Queen*, and how the children refuse or acknowledge these sensations and pleasures, shows us how the Native child's body might be an important site for responding to colonization.

I explore *Kiss of the Fur Queen* in particular because, as a piece of indigenous literature, it can "supplement forgetting with new narratives of affirmation and presence" (Lowe 2015: 40). Violent colonization continues into the present, but the rhetoric of the modern-day nation-state obscures the history and presence of violence, often masking it as care, thus producing what Lisa Lowe calls a "violence of . . . forgetting" (ibid.: 41). Indigenous literature makes us recognize that *not everyone has forgotten*. Despite ongoing colonization, indigenous communities *do survive*, and literature is one site where indigenous peoples can affirm their survival, presence, and remembering. Lowe uses the historian Stephanie Smallwood's statement that "I try to imagine what could have been" as a jumping-off point to consider how "the *past condition temporality* of the 'what could have been' symbolizes aptly the space of a different kind of thinking, a space of productive attention to the scene of loss" (40–41). I suggest that indigenous literature is a site where the "what could have been" is imaginatively and productively enacted to resist the settler state's imperative to forget.[5]

Indigenous literature that depicts sexuality participates in both a resistance to forgetting and a refusal of erasure. Daniel Heath Justice (2008: 103) explains that "as indigenousness itself has long been a colonialist target, so too has our joy, our desire, our sense of ourselves as being able to both give and receive pleasure." Justice asserts that seemingly quotidian bodily experiences and affects— "joy," "desire," "pleasure"—are not isolated from but intimately tied up

with settler colonialism; paying attention to these sensations, especially in literature, then, is a way to track and potentially resist the violence of settler colonialism on the ground. Since "Aboriginal peoples [are viewed] as historical artifacts,
degraded vagrants or grieving ghosts," "to take joy in our bodies—and those bodies in relation to others—is to strike out against five hundred plus years of disregard, disrespect, and dismissal" (ibid.: 104). Here, Justice connects being viewed
as remnant anachronisms—"artifacts," "vagrants," "ghosts"—to being viewed as
without bodies or without sexualities. Asserting sexuality is a way to assert presence, resist erasure, and combat the narrative that views Natives as disappeared
or their sexuality as damaged. Justice sees writing about these experiences as a
way to enact resistance: "Our sexuality isn't just part of our Nativeness—it's fuel
for the healing of our nations" (ibid.: 106). Representing Native sexuality in literature, then, depicts sensations at the micro-level that have potential to combat
macro-level violences and enable pathways toward "healing."

Highway's fictional text initially started as a memoir, based on his own
time in a residential school in Canada. The story's final form as a novel allows it to
imagine a "what could have been" that permits us to approach some of the vexed
issues surrounding Native queer childhood. Linking fiction to social change, Sam
McKegney (2005: 81) examines how Native fiction and Highway's text in particular
enact political resistance in ways that differ from memoir or testimonial because
it can "unsettle comfortable power relations by creatively reimagining Indigenous
culture and identity in the contemporary moment." Focus on the "contemporary
moment" is crucial because of the ongoing legacy and ramifications of the boarding school, which is arguably most visible in the modern-day foster care system
disproportionately made up of Native children; Native children continue to be targets of state intervention into Native kinship and futurity.[6]

The novel is a fictional account of the Cree brothers Champion and Oonee-
meetoo, who are christened Jeremiah and Gabriel and forced to use these names
when they attend an Indian boarding school run by Catholic priests in the 1960s
and 1970s. The novel is divided into six parts, and we follow the boys throughout
their childhoods, first in northern Manitoba and then in the boarding school, as
well as their adulthoods in Winnipeg, when Jeremiah becomes an accomplished
pianist and Gabriel a successful dancer who identifies as a gay man.[7] An omni-
scient narrator gives us access to their diverging trajectories and also introduces us
to the Fur Queen, the trickster figure who watches over and confronts the boys at
moments when the settler world is severing them from their Native roots. Highway's
choice to tell the story about two brothers, who are fated to different experiences
in the text, allows him to render two plots that differently present and imagine the

effects of queer Native childhood. While *The Kiss of the Fur Queen* is a sweeping and rich text, I focus mainly on the boys' time in the boarding school and where I see it affecting their adulthood to think through some of these effects.

In the boarding school, Gabriel and Jeremiah are educated in the rhythms of what J. Jack Halberstam (2005: 5) terms "repro-time," learning the proper practices that will enable heterosexual reproduction and (white) futurity. Education about repro-time is not recruitment into repro-time, and this distinction becomes clear once the boys pass through the school. Nonetheless, the school works to ensure that the bodies that pass through it are successfully internalizing this education in repro-time. The school carefully monitors the body and particularly its interactions with the opposite sex. When Jeremiah arrives at school, "his sisters . . . were marched away to their own world the minute they got off the plane" (Highway 1998: 64). At school, "girls had their own yard . . . away from the view of lusty lads" (ibid.: 63). The "lusty lads" are the school-aged boy children, and enforcing this separation of boys and girls works to teach children the appropriate object to desire while implying that this desire is inappropriate and must be prevented through strict separation. In this way, the school constructs heterosexuality as the appropriate end for children while teaching the children that desire is not permitted in this heterosexual paradigm. Rifkin (2011: 147) understands this construction to be a crucial component in the "romance plot" that the school narrates—schools "regulate social interaction between the sexes . . . [and] orchestrate and manage the process of courting" (ibid.: 152). More than just "orchestrating and manag[ing]" this process, they *produce* it through their regulations. Building on this connection between the disciplinary productions of heterosexuality and its accompanying affects in Native bodies, Deborah Miranda (2002: 140) notes that "the strict separation of boys and girls during long stints at Indian Boarding School . . . not only changed Native courtship and coming-of-age experiences, but also inscribed a European, Christianized dogma regarding the 'dirtiness' of Native bodies and sexuality in general." Educating children in "courtship" and heterosexual practices necessitated teaching children how to look back on "Native bodies and sexuality" as "dirty." Producing gendered categories and teaching appropriate romantic and sexual affect and behavior worked to queer the Native body and produce shame and disavowal of sexuality. Children were taught what a heterosexual future looked like, but sexual orphanings would preclude them from gaining access to that future.

Thus, the production and structuring of appropriate desire was not in the service of making sure that Native children would heterosexually reproduce. After the boarding school, it is impossible for Jeremiah to return home, at least geo-graphically—"he had absolutely nowhere to go" (Highway 1998: 103). He settles in Winnipeg, where "in this metropolis of half a million souls . . . he seemed to be the only Indian person" (ibid.: 100). Isolated and demarcated from the whiteness surrounding him, Jeremiah is left extricated from his Native community. While on a bus in this city, Jeremiah remembers how the school monitored "every bodily secretion" (ibid.: 102); conjoined with this memory of surveillance is the realiza-tion that in this city, unlike the school, he was "free to talk to girls. Except that there were no girls to talk to. At his [current high] school, there may have been a thousand, but they were all white" (ibid.: 102). Since Indian reproductivity can-not cross racialized lines, the heterosexual desire in which Jeremiah has been educated cannot be enacted outside the school. The girls he has been oriented to desire "were all white" and thus inaccessible to his Native body. This illusory, constructed "romance plot" halts the possibility of a future generation of Natives.

Despite being barred from repro-time, Jeremiah cannot unlearn this edu-cation that privileges the "biological clock . . . [and] bourgeois rules" (Halbers-tam 2005: 5). As an adult, he comes face-to-face with the Fur Queen, the larger-than-life embodiment of Cree culture who has "no gender" and structures the text; the trickster asks him what the point of life is, to which Jeremiah responds, "You are born. You grow up, you go to school, you work—you work like hell—you get married, sometimes, you raise a family, sometimes, you grow old. And then you die" (Highway 1998: vii, 233). This understanding of life follows the "biological" and "bourgeois" markers that are characteristic of repro-time, recognizing a clear beginning (birth) and end (death) punctuated by heteronormative life events (mar-riage and family). The mandate of marriage and family is twice-spliced by a per-haps hesitant, perhaps qualifying "sometimes," which might illustrate Jeremiah's recognition that he himself will not participate in this heterotime. The boarding school has cultivated within Jeremiah an understanding of what existence *should* look like according to a linear, heterosexual model; at no point in the text, however, does he achieve these heteronormative milestones.

The settler state successfully queers Jeremiah through educating him in straightness. He is educated in a reproductive futurism in which he can never participate. This ban queers him because he is, in the conclusion that José Este-ban Muñoz (2009) recognizes as that of many children of color, never able to grow up. Jeremiah is unable to move forward but unable to return home, temporally, sexually, or in terms of kinship. He, then, is orphaned from sexuality—enabled by an orphaning from his Native past and resulting in an orphaning from a potential reproductive future; his experience and education in the school have left him with a Native body from which he is disconnected. Native queer childhood bars Jeremiah from the future.

The Sovereign Erotic and Erotics
of Sovereignty in *Kiss of the Fur Queen*

The sexual orphanings that Jeremiah experiences differ from those of Gabriel, who is raped by a white priest, Father Lafleur, during his time at the school. Jeremiah is left orphaned from his sexuality; however, the abuse Gabriel experiences produces sensations that alter the totalizing effects of his orphaning. Gabriel's sexuality both as a child and as an adult is inextricably linked with and perhaps even a product of his experience of sexual abuse—elements present in the scene the first time the priest rapes him are also present in his adult homosexual encounters. While the sexual abuse that Father Lafleur commits asserts colonial control over the bodies of Native children, the scenes of violence present abuse alongside sensations of pleasure.[8]

I use Qwo-Li Driskill's concept of the sovereign erotic to think about how ownership over one's body might paradoxically come through damage. Driskill (2004: 50) writes, "We were stolen from our bodies / We were stolen from our homes," and defines the sovereign erotic as "an erotic wholeness healed and/or healing from the historical trauma that First Nations people continue to survive, rooted within the histories, traditions, and resistance struggles of our nations" (ibid.: 51). For Driskill, the sovereign erotic allows for an "erotic wholeness" even after being "stolen"—or orphaned—from the Native body. While Driskill envisions an "erotic wholeness," I am interested in how the body might heal in ways that do not necessarily result in wholeness but nonetheless open up pathways for decolonization. *Kiss of the Fur Queen* gives us a way to consider if and how local features of the body that constitute the erotic—bodily sensations and pleasures—disturb the totalizing narrative and violence of settler colonialism.

Thinking of decolonization happening at the level of individual bodies, and more specifically at the level of erotics, challenges the way we think about scale. These erotics are what M. Jacqui Alexander (2005: 297, 329) might term types of "body praxis," practices and sensations that "position . . . the body as a source of knowledge within terms differently modulated than the materiality of the body and its entanglement in the struggle against commodification." Alexander focuses on spiritual rituals that engage the body as the "means through which we come to be at home in the body that supersede its positioning in materiality, in any of the

violent discourses of appropriation, and in any of the formations within normative multiculturalism" (ibid.: 329). In other words, the spiritual is one register for
accessing a relation to the body, finding a "home in the body," that is otherwise
foreclosed. I use Alexander to think not of the spiritual but of the physical, and
specifically the erotic, as a way to approach how the body might act as a source of
knowledge that exceeds the education produced in institutions, enabling ways to
inhabit the body against which the state educates.[9]

Alexander's formulation of the body as home is especially salient when
thinking about Native boarding-school children; Driskill (2004: 53) argues that
the body "is the first homeland" and one of many homes from which Native children are orphaned. This conceptualization of "home" is not strictly geographi-
cally determined or rooted to land; it is an expansive understanding of "home"
that takes seriously the body's role and allows us to consider the relation between
Alexander's "radical self-possession" and the dispossession of Native land. In
other words, settler colonialism dispossesses Native Americans not just of their
land but also of their bodies through a violent education that imposes settler sexuality and teaches children to apprehend erotics as shameful. Rifkin (2011: 151)
explains that the settler state requires that "to gain 'individuality' [a necessity for
white understandings of property and land ownership] Indians must shift the horizon of their thinking and, more importantly, their feeling, connecting 'home' not
to specific tribal territories but to the great expanse of the entire United States."
Children are educated to abandon attachment to "specific tribal territories" and
understand "home" as a "great expanse," one that will never welcome them. The
reality of colonization makes a return to "home" in terms of kinship and geography
impossible—some orphanings are irreversible. However, if the body can serve as
a "home" through a reclamation of erotics that the schools disallow, decolonization
might begin to occur at the level of individual bodies.

Gabriel's abuse and the pleasure it produces enable him to maintain a
connection to the Native body despite abuse. His reaction to the abuse and how
this first sexual violation recurs during his lifetime reveal that within traumatic,
sexual violence, there is space for him to disrupt the sexual orphanings that this
abuse works to incur. Embracing the pleasure produced in these encounters allows
him to *return home through the body*. This return is not a temporal one; he is not
returning to some pristine Indian past untouched by colonial violence. Gabriel
returns to a body that has been violated and colonized, but allowing himself to
experience pleasure and sensation—the very bodily practices the school produces
in order to shame—enables a connection to the sovereign erotic that heals.

The first violation in *Kiss of the Fur Queen* is bound with and even contingent on Gabriel's pleasure. Gabriel performs in a school play and "beamed with pleasure" (Highway 1998: 76) as he dances across the stage, where an audience that includes Father Lafleur watches him. When Gabriel sleeps later that night, he dreams that he is dancing and that his "little body was moving up and down . . . producing, in the crux of his being, a sensation so pleasurable," but upon awaking, "the face of the principal loomed inches from [Gabriel's] own" (ibid.: 77). This sequence of events reveals that it is the performative act of dancing—an act that produced "pleasure" within Gabriel—that triggers Father Lafleur to approach Gabriel's bed that evening. Gabriel's pleasure, then, comes prior to the priest's and is actually responsible for the priest's own pleasure. Native sexuality takes precedence—the young Gabriel has not been rid of his sexuality yet, nor is it something primitive and in the past; his sexuality is present and powerful and apprehended as a sensation "in the crux of his being."

When Gabriel wakes up and realizes what is happening to him, his experience of pleasure disrupts the power dynamics of the encounter. The description of the rape that occurs reveals that Gabriel, while a victim, is not a passive object onto whom the priest inflicts violence during the act:

> From some tinny radio somewhere off . . . [Gabriel] could hear Elvis Presley singing 'Love Me Tender' . . . Gradually, Father Lafleur bent, closer and closer, until the crucifix that dangled from his neck came to rest on Gabriel's face. The subtly throbbing motion of the priest's upper body made the naked Jesus Christ—this sliver of silver light, this fleshly Son of God so achingly beautiful—rub his body against the child's lips, over and over and over again. Gabriel had no strength left. The pleasure in his centre welled so deep that he was about to open his mouth and swallow whole the living flesh—in his half-dream state, this man nailed to the cross was a living, breathing man, tasting like Gabriel's most favourite food, warm honey. (Highway 1998: 78–79)

While Gabriel sees himself as an object over whom "holy men" have a "right" (ibid.: 78), this passage depicts an unexpected consequence of that right: the "pleasure" in Gabriel's "centre [that] welled so deep." Highway's narration of this pleasure forces us to pause and consider how to account for pleasure, and specifically sexual pleasure in a child, in a scene of vivid, unquestionable violence. Acknowledging the presence of this pleasure is crucial, even if uncomfortable. As Justice (2008: 106) asserts, "To ignore sex and embodied pleasure in the cause of Indigenous liberation is to ignore one of our greatest resources. . . . Every orgasm can be an act of decolonization." The presence of sexual pleasure in an act of sexual violation suggests the potential for the sovereign erotic and the "resource" of pleasure. Gabriel's pleasure disrupts the attempted colonization and orphaning of his body by creating space for and allowing the erotic.

Allowing for the erotic means that Gabriel is not orphaning it; the sexual orphaning on which the state depends fails. Audre Lorde ([1984] 2007: 53) argues that Western conceptualizations of sexuality, particularly as they are tied with "suppression," interfere with an ability to see the erotic as a site and "source of power and information." Connecting with rather than suppressing the erotic, acknowledging rather than refusing the erotic, enables Natives to retain and reclaim what colonizers have attempted to destroy and restructure. If erasing the erotic is part of the colonization and queering of Native communities, connecting to and allowing the erotic functions as an important step toward decolonization. It also allows the possibility to reclaim or heal ties with Native conceptualizations of sexuality, thus resisting the state's project of queering and rendering backward Native cultures.

Importantly, the erotic is not limited to the domain of sexuality. Lorde explains how it involves the political, spiritual, emotional, and social spheres, and Driskill (2004: 52) reiterates this point when they explain that the erotic is "not . . . a realm of personal consequence only. Our relationships with the erotic impact our larger communities, just as our communities impact our sense of the erotic. A Sovereign Erotic relates our bodies to our nations, traditions, and histories." Thus Gabriel's erotic encounter with the priest, even though "confusi[ng]" for him, helps him maintain a crucial connection to his "nation, traditions, and histories" (Highway 1998: 78). His pleasure interrupts a complete sexual orphaning.

Once he leaves the school, Gabriel experiences sexual pleasure as an adult, and these experiences invoke elements from his initial sexual encounter with Father Lafleur. After joining Jeremiah in the south, Gabriel almost immediately has sex with a man who was "transported by [his] cool beauty. . . . Ulysses' sirens had begun to sing 'Love Me Tender' and the Cree Adonis could taste, upon the buds that lined his tongue, warm honey" (Highway 1998: 120–21). The return of the song "Love Me Tender" and the honey in this new sexual encounter suggest that his traumatic experience is shaping his adult sexuality. Elements of this first encounter continue to crop up in his sexual experiences outside the boarding school, especially "the naked Jesus Christ" crucifix the priest is wearing the first time he rapes Gabriel.[10]

Ann Cvetkovich (2003: 102) offers a way to begin to see the recurrence of trauma as a site of potentiality. She asserts that there can be "unpredictable potential [in] traumatic experience." She seeks a conceptualization of trauma that is "not pathologize[d]" but "that forge[s] creative responses" (ibid.: 3). The "creative" responses may, then, link sexual trauma to the "creative" power of the erotic—both are capable of opening up new spaces. She is particularly interested in the productive power of flashbacks. Flashbacks, characterized by the fact that they force a subject to repeat a traumatic event, may contain "subversive possi- bilities of repetition with a difference" (ibid.: 74). In other words, if an experi- ence can be repeated but part of the experience can be changed or altered, it may "provide the basis for healing rituals and performances . . . [which] exemplifies Eve Sedgwick's notion of a queer 'shame-creativity,' which reclaims that which has been debased and repudiated" (ibid.). "Embracing rather than refusing" trauma can actually be a way to heal from it (ibid.). It can counter sexual orphanings through this "shame-creativity." The very repetition of trauma and the fact that it brings the past into the present might help counter the temporal orphanings that the school enforces; it disrupts the normal unfolding of the forward timeline, creat- ing a space in which to "grow sideways."

Gabriel grows up to identify as a gay man, a description of same-sex desire that is an effect of his induction into a modern settler sexuality. In an argument during which his brother, Jeremiah, realizes that Gabriel is gay, Jeremiah says, "How can you let someone do what that disgusting old priest did to you? How can you seek out . . . people like that?" to which Gabriel responds, "And you? . . . You'd rather diddle with a piano than diddle with yourself. You're dead. . . . At least my body is still alive" (Highway 1998: 207). While Jeremiah has "willed his body dead" (ibid.: 205), Gabriel's body is "alive," and being alive allows him to experi- ence sexual pleasure and erotic power. That he qualifies this survival of his body with "at least" might dwarf the impact of this survival; however, colonization and education have orphaned Gabriel from much of his Indianness, and he sees how in his brother, "Kill the Indian" has succeeded in killing the Native body. Gabri- el's body's survival, then, is an individual site that has remained alive in the face of ongoing violent assault. In this moment, we see definitively that the traumatic violence of the boarding school does not succeed in orphaning Gabriel from his sexuality—rather, it keeps him connected to it and alive.

The final scene shows us how this healing enables Gabriel's survival in an alternative time and space through the trickster narrative. Gabriel is diagnosed with AIDS in his early adult life, a diagnosis that indicates that his life will be cut short and that he will not participate in the reproductive order; he is the tar- get of multiple genocides.[11] While he is on his deathbed, "the Fur Queen swept

into the room. . . . Rising from his body, Gabriel Okimasis and the Fur Queen
floated off into the swirling mist" (Highway 1998: 306). Gabriel "ris[es] from his
body," leaving behind the Indian body from which the settler state so vehemently
tried to alienate him. The scene suggests that while his body is left behind, his
subjectivity continues—upon leaving his body, he can still "float off." The settler
state has attempted to educate Gabriel to orphan his own sexuality. Highway imagines Gabriel's refusal to orphan his sexuality, and this imagining enables a final
scene where Gabriel can orphan his own body but still survive. A connection to his
body enabled by orphanings enables his return home, which requires him to leave
behind that body and go with the trickster. Highway explains that the "continued
presence of this extraordinary figure" of the trickster prevents "the core of Indian
culture [from] be[ing] gone forever" (ibid.: vii). The final image of Gabriel and the
trickster is one of survival and continuance not bound to linear time or material
space, and still able to emerge despite fractures caused by sexual orphanings.
Gabriel is denied the future, but Highway imagines an alternate way to endure.
Kiss of the Fur Queen offers some possibilities for what "growing sideways" might
look like—it is a site of pleasure and repetition, full of potentiality and continuance even if not future oriented.

When Queerness Is Not Liberatory

Recent exchanges between queer and indigenous studies have been marked by
productive tensions around issues such as kinship, institutions, pleasure, reproduction, and temporality. Both fields critique the state's management of bodies and
sexualities for the purpose of excluding queer and Native communities from state-
sanctioned futures, exclusions that have been justified by rendering both Natives
and queers in similar temporal terms: backward and childlike. However, key and
revealing differences have emerged, for instance, in divergent views of kinship.
While queer studies tends toward a utopic view of alternative kinship structures,
indigenous studies reminds us that intervening into kinship, coupled with the production of queer kinship in Native communities, has been a violent tactic used by
the settler state to access and steal Native land over the last two centuries. Queer
studies attends to pleasure, rejects normativity, and embraces nonreproductivity,
but indigenous studies asks us how these issues must be taken up differently in
the face of ongoing cultural and biological genocide. Native people have not disappeared, but the attempts to disappear them make reproductivity salient and not
something we can easily dismiss. In other words, queer studies' embrace of plea-

sure and nonreproductivity can happen when there is a guarantee that bodies and populations will be there and will reproduce and survive; queer studies has limits in an indigenous context where survival and futurity are at stake.

In this essay, I have turned to the children of boarding schools as especially charged figures through whom to consider these historical and theoretical tensions at the intersection of queer and indigenous studies. This argument has taken a seemingly nonqueer approach to reproduction by casting it as a litmus test for viewing how the settler state prevents Natives from accessing the future, thus aligning reproduction and the future. However, Native children are not synonymous with or guaranteed a future in the context of settler colonialism; in fact, I argue that promises of futurity to Native children in the form of education obscure violences intended to prevent that very future. Second, since the settler state saw Native bodies as an obstacle to the seizure of land, legal and otherwise, preventing the literal reproduction of Native populations was crucial to settler expansion; taking seriously Native reproduction allows us to track how the settler state attempted to prevent the expansion of Native populations through sexual education of their children. My argument reveals the double bind of Indian education: children were educated to understand and experience their Indianness as queer, and thus orphaned from it, and then they were educated in white heterosexual norms, norms in which they would always fail because of their race. Paradoxically, then, ostensible heterosexuality queers these children. Queer, here, is not liberatory but genocidal. The settler state's refusal of the future to Natives is not liberatory but genocidal. And the promise of a future—through education—is a false one that enables this queering.

Notes

I would like to thank the editors of this volume for all the time and energy they invested in this work. I am grateful to Heather Love, Bethany Schneider, and Kate Thomas for their generous mentorship and generative feedback on this piece. Thank you to Scott Herring and all the participants at Indiana Bloomington's "Child Matters" conference for their critical engagement with this work. Many thanks to the anonymous reviewers for their attentive comments and helpful suggestions.

1.   Robin Bernstein (2011: 16) has done exceptional work on how innocence is preserved for white children, while racialized children, and particularly African American children, are viewed as incapable of that innocence and thus "exclu[ded] . . . from the category of childhood."

2.   While practices and understandings varied from nation to nation, the settler state

homogenized these practices, seeing them all as deviant. This pan-Native outlook extended to the schools, where children from many nations resided. Interactions between members of the same nation were strictly monitored so as to prevent attachment and allegiance to the communities from which they came; for example, children from the same tribe would be separated to make sure they were not speaking their language.

3. In this same *GLQ* issue, Andrea Smith (2010: 51) emphasizes the "eternal" element of this project, noting that "the Native is rendered permanently infantile . . . an innocent savage. She cannot mature into adult citizenship, she can only be locked into a permanent state of infancy." If Natives are "permanently infantile," then both the present and "future of the white, settler citizen" (Smith 2005: 51) are always guaranteed—and the future of Native communities is always tied up with and in the service of this white future. Natives must remain in this orphaned state in order for "white, settler citizen[s]" to maintain their destructive and dominating acts over Native land and bodies.

4. While I argue that the schools demonstrate that the state's intent was never to actually assimilate these children or grant them full access to a settler future, a range of agents worked in and for these schools. It is likely that many did not know what they were participating in and indeed probably thought that they were helping these children. I point this out to show how structural, macro-level design of the school enabled a mission that those operating on the micro-level—in the schools and classrooms—helped purport, regardless of individual intention.

5. Rifkin also sees indigenous writing about sexuality as a way to productively engage with the "what could have been." Building on Craig Womack's (2008) critical formulation of imagining as vital for the production of Native epistemologies, Rifkin (2012, 27) asks if "the erotic might serve as a source of imagination? . . . Creative engagement with the erotic can . . . register . . . the largely unacknowledged presence of the past as well as opening heretofore (officially) unrecognized potentials for living indigeneity in the present." In other words, imagining an erotics that exceeds those mandated by settler sexuality opens up "potentials" for Natives in the present. Thus, Highway's rendering of the sexual orphanings in the 1960s boarding school in a 1998 fictional text has ramifications for available indigenous modes of being in the present.

6. Deborah Miranda (2002: 138) observes that "separation from parents and extended family resulted in adult survivors of boarding school who had no idea how to parent." Lisa Poupart (2003: 93) explains how this proliferation of "unparented parents" has been further complicated by "the erosion of traditional extended-family systems . . . [which means] many are without the traditional networks of emotional and economic support." The boarding schools' intervention into kinship coupled with lack of institutional support has not completely halted Native reproduction, but it has altered and limited what the Native family and community can look like today.

7. Highway is a survivor of the boarding school system in Canada—there are certainly significant differences between the US settler state and the Canadian settler state, but the school systems developed and functioned similarly; McKegney (2005: 79) notes that "like American boarding schools, Canadian residential schools acted as a weapon in a calculated attack on Indigenous cultures." I use this text to think about a broader Native North American experience of boarding/residential school and its effects, which opens up ways for thinking about transnational indigeneity.

8. Rifkin (2014: 140) has recently explored how the text "perform[s] an erotohistoriography of indigeneity and settler colonialism," drawing on Lynda Hart to examine how the "incorporation of [Gabriel's] abuse into his sexuality provides a means of challenging 'the dominant order's symbolic,' refusing the negation of Indigenous eroticism." My reading aligns in part with Rifkin's, who suggests that this incorporation resists the erasure of Native sexuality. However, Rifkin focuses on how the text maintains and "reimagine[s] Indigenous continuity" (ibid.) and tradition, while I read the text as resulting in orphanings, which are forms of noncontinuity, that nonetheless open up ways for considering indigenous sexuality.

9. This is not to say that erotics do not include the domain of the spiritual—later in this essay, I engage with Audre Lorde's ([1984] 2007) famous definition of the erotic in order to think about how reconnecting with a disavowed erotic has implications beyond the domain of the physical; however, I am interested in investigating exactly how the sensations, pleasures, and bodily practices that constitute erotics can function as sources of knowledge before making this move.

10. Instances where we see the recurrence of these elements in Highway 1998: 132, 169, 185, 204, and 263.

11. In *Epistemology of the Closet*, Eve Kosofsky Sedgwick ([1990] 2008: 130) states that AIDS is "unlike genocide directed against Jews, Native Americans, Africans, or other groups" because "gay genocide, the once-and-for-all eradication of gay populations . . . is not possible short of the eradication of the whole human species." While Sedgwick counterposes the genocides against Native Americans and gay persons because of her understanding of how Native and gay identities emerge, Highway proposes seeing Native and gay genocide as intertwined in *Kiss of the Fur Queen*. Both are genocides enacted on queered populations, and as a gay Native American, Gabriel occupies the position of the child queered by Native genocide who will be queered by AIDS.

References

Alexander, M. Jacqui. 2005. *Pedagogies of Crossing: Meditation on Feminism, Sexual Politics, Memory, and the Sacred.* Durham, NC: Duke University Press.

Berlant, Lauren. 2011. *Cruel Optimism.* Durham, NC: Duke University Press.

Bernstein, Robin. 2011. *Racial Innocence: Performing American Childhood from Slavery to Civil Rights.* New York: New York University Press.

Bruhm, Steven, and Natasha Hurley, eds. 2004. *Curiouser: On the Queerness of Children.* Minneapolis: University of Minnesota Press.

Castronovo, Russ. 2001. *Necro Citizenship: Death, Eroticism, and the Public Sphere in the Nineteenth-Century United States.* Durham, NC: Duke University Press.

Cvetkovich, Ann. 2003. *Archive of Feelings: Trauma, Sexuality, and Lesbian Public Cultures.* Durham, NC: Duke University Press.

———. 2012. *Depression: A Public Feeling.* Durham, NC: Duke University Press.

DeJong, David. 2007. "'Unless They Are Kept Alive': Federal Indian Schools and Student Health, 1878–1918." *American Indian Quarterly* 31, no. 2: 256–82.

———. 2008. *If You Knew the Conditions: A Chronicle of the Indian Medical Service and American Indian Health Care, 1908–1955.* Lanham, MD: Lexington Books.

Driskill, Qwo-Li. 2004. "Stolen from Our Bodies: First Nation Two Spirits / Queers and the Journey to a Sovereign Erotic." *Studies in American Indian Literatures* 16, no. 2: 50–64.

Edelman, Lee. 2004. *No Future: Queer Theory and the Death Drive.* Durham, NC: Duke University Press.

Finley, Chris. 2011. "Decolonizing the Queer Native Body (and Recovering the Native Bull-Dyke): Bringing 'Sexy Back' and Out of Native Studies' Closet." In *Queer Indigenous Studies*, edited by Qwo-Li Driskill, Chris Finley, Brian Joseph Gilley, and Scott Morgensen, 31–42. Tucson: University of Arizona Press.

Foucault, Michel. [1976] 2003. *"Society Must Be Defended": Lectures at the College de France, 1975–1976.* Translated by David Macey. New York: Picador.

Halberstam, J. Jack. 2005. *In a Queer Time and Place.* New York: New York University Press.

Highway, Tomson. 1998. *Kiss of the Fur Queen.* Norman: University of Oklahoma Press.

Jacobs, Margaret. 2009. *White Mother to a Dark Race: Settler Colonialism, Maternalism, and the Removal of Indigenous Children in the American West and Australia, 1880–1940.* Lincoln: University of Nebraska Press.

Justice, Daniel Heath. 2008. "Fear of a Changeling Moon: A Rather Queer Tale from a Cherokee Hillbilly." In *Me Sexy: An Exploration of Native Sex and Sexuality*, edited by Drew Hayden Taylor, 87–108. Vancouver: Douglas and McIntyre.

Lorde, Audre. [1978] 2007. "Uses of the Erotic: The Erotic as Power." In *Sister Outsider: Essays and Speeches by Audre Lorde*, 53–59. Berkeley, CA: Crossing Press.

Lowe, Lisa. 2015. *The Intimacies of Four Continents.* Durham, NC: Duke University Press.

McKegney, Sam. 2005. "From Trickster Discourses to Transgressive Politics." *Studies in American Indian Literature* 17: 79–113.

Miranda, Deborah A. 2002. "Dildos, Hummingbirds, and Driving Her Crazy: Searching for American Indian Women's Love Poetry and Erotics." *Frontiers* 23, no. 2: 135–49.

Morgensen, Scott Lauria. 2010. "Settler Homonationalism: Theorizing Settler Colonialism within Queer Modernities." *GLQ* 16, nos. 1–2: 105–31.

Muñoz, José Esteban. 2009. *Cruising Utopia: The Then and There of Queer Futurity.* New York: New York University Press.

Poupart, Lisa M. 2003. "The Familiar Face of Genocide: Internalized Oppression among American Indians." *Hypatia* 18, no. 2: 86–100.

Pratt, Richard H. [1908] 1979. *The Indian Industrial School, Carlisle, Pennsylvania: Its Origins, Purposes, Progress, and the Difficulties Surmounted.* Carlisle, PA: Cumberland County Historical Society.

Puar, Jasbir. 2011. "The Cost of Getting Better: Suicide, Sensation, Switchpoints." *GLQ* 18, no. 1: 149–58.

Rhoades, Everett. 1976. *Report on Indian Health, Task Force Six: Final Report to the American Indian Policy Review Commission.* Washington, DC: Government Printing Office.

Rifkin, Mark. 2011. *When Did Indians Become Straight? Kinship, the History of Sexuality, and Native Sovereignty.* New York: Oxford University Press.

———. 2012. *Erotics of Sovereignty.* Minneapolis: University of Minnesota Press.

———. 2014. "Queering Indigenous Pasts, or Temporalities of Tradition and Settlement." In *The Oxford Handbook of Indigenous American Literature,* edited by James H. Cox and Daniel Heath Justice, 137–51. Oxford: Oxford University Press.

Rogin, Michael. [1975] 2008. *Fathers and Children: Andrew Jackson and the Subjugation of the American Indian.* New Brunswick, NJ: Transaction.

Schneider, Bethany. 2010. "Introduction: Bethany's Take." *GLQ* 16, nos. 1–2: 13–22.

———. 2015. "A Modest Proposal: Laura Ingalls Wilder Ate Zitkala-Ša." *GLQ* 21, no. 1: 65–93.

Sedgwick, Eve Kosofsky. [1990] 2008. *Epistemology of the Closet.* Berkeley: University of California Press.

Smith, Andrea. 2005. *Conquest: Sexual Violence and American Indian Genocide.* Cambridge, MA: South End.

———. 2010. "Queer Theory and Native Studies: The Heteronormativity of Settler Colonialism." *GLQ* 16, nos. 1–2: 41–68.

Stockton, Kathryn Bond. 2009. *The Queer Child, or Growing Sideways in the Twentieth Century.* Durham, NC: Duke University Press.

Wolfe, Patrick. 2006. "Settler Colonialism and the Elimination of the Native." *Journal of Genocide Research* 8, no. 4: 387–409.

Womack, Craig. 2008. "Theorizing American Indian Experience." In *Reasoning Together: The Native Critics Collective,* edited by Craig Womack, Daniel Heath Justice, and Christopher Teuton, 353–410. Norman: University of Oklahoma Press.

BIOPOWER BELOW
AND BEFORE THE INDIVIDUAL

Kyla Schuller

Testo Junkie: Sex, Drugs, and Biopolitics in the Pharmacopornographic Era
Paul B. Preciado, translated by Bruce Benderson
New York: Feminist Press, 2013. x + 427 pp.

The Exquisite Corpse of Asian America:
Biopolitics, Biosociality, and Posthuman Ecologies
Rachel C. Lee
New York: New York University Press, 2014. vi + 325 pp.

Racial Indigestion: Eating Bodies in the Nineteenth Century
Kyla Wazana Tompkins
New York: New York University Press, 2012. xiv + 276 pp.

*A*fter being arrested in 1952 for public indecency and sexual perversion, Alan Turing was sentenced to estrogen injections that the Hollywood film *Imitation Game* (Tyldum 2014) portrays as destroying his manhood as well as his mind. Homosexuality was coincident with Turing's greatness, *The Imitation Game* insists, but endogenous hormones were intrinsic to his brilliance.[1] Yet the film also offers a glimpse into the larger political machinery in which Turing operated, a system that new queer studies scholarship on biopower helps illuminate. This broader frame renders Turing a figure unwittingly located at the nexus of three major vectors of Foucauldian biopower: the emergence of the homosexual as a medical-juridical subject, the administration of the population through the calculation of risk, and

GLQ 22:4
DOI 10.1215/10642684-3603126
© 2016 by Duke University Press

the circulation of hormones as tactics of securitization. Turing had helped devise both a foolproof method of decoding Nazi communiqués and a systematic approach to choosing when to redirect targeted Allied missions away from the impending attack. There could not be a starker image of biopolitics: the rational computation of risk that sacrificed the majority of Allied sailors for the benefit of the war effort as a whole, which the film's most poetic line extols as Turing's "blood-soaked calculus." Less than a decade later, however, Turing became a participant in another key development in biopower—the invention of medicalized gender—though this time he figured among the condemned. Midcentury medical and pharmacological techniques, Paul B. Preciado argues, led to the rise of the biomedical subjectivity "gender" as well as the broad circulation of hormones among the population: estrogen was soon to become the most widely marketed pharmaceutical molecule in history. Turing himself chose one year of estrogen treatment, also known as "chemical castration," as an alternative to jail time, and although he complained of the resultant gynecomastia, he continued his work apace (Copeland 2014). Turing was thus not only the victim of the hormonal treatment of homosexuality but also a coerced participant in the rise of medicalized gender.

The books reviewed here, Preciado's *Testo Junkie*, Kyla Wazana Tompkins's *Racial Indigestion*, and Rachel C. Lee's *Exquisite Corpse*, signal a significant turn in biopolitical theory. In this scholarship we can see the emergence of a third biopolitical entity, one that plays a key role in Turing's story. We might call the entity materializing in recent queer-feminist work "force." Force materializes within and alongside the two social formations Michel Foucault named: the individual and the population. The individual is the product of disciplinary personhood, of the orchestration of social space to manage the individual organism, while the population is understood to be a biological phenomenon in its own right, characterized by rates of birth, death, illness, and economic productivity that become the very tactics of its administration. Force comprises affects, molecules, morsels, organs, microbes, animacies, tissues, cells, hormones, energies, textures, apertures, calories, pheromones, stimulations, and other particles and intensities that circulate throughout the individual, population, and milieu. Force exists adjacent to and within the administrative vectors of the individual and the population, circulating throughout a milieu independently, accumulating within and as persons, and forming links among matter that forge bodies and populations.[2] Force helps turn a space into a milieu, an environment in which species and objects affect one another, even at a distance. Force aggregates as gender and racial difference, through the extraction and traffic in particles and vitalities that flow in and out of individual bodies and national populations, such as the increased estrogen streaming through Turing's body.[3] Across these three books, regulating, marketizing, and optimizing the flow of force emerges as a key function of biopower.

Among these three texts, Lee, a literary scholar, is the most direct in proposing a third vector of biopolitical administration and pointing to its intellectual yield. Her impressively multidisciplinary reading of Asian Americanist cultural production and feminist science studies tracks what she calls "the tripartite scales of biosociality—the scale of the person, the scale of the microbe, and the scale of the population" (30). She does so to interrogate the meaning of racial embodiment in the contemporary bioeconomy. *The Exquisite Corpse* explores how the scale of the microbe affects preexisting notions of race rooted in epidermal difference. Contemporary capitalism, for Nikolas Rose and others, depends partly on fragmenting personhood into marketable tissues, cells, and microbes distributed throughout discrete times and spaces, and as such, scholars must attend to the subindividual circuits of biological material. Building on this work, Lee asks: can critical race studies profitably attend to the level of power that circulates below the level of the human, which fragments the biological, a circuit that may or may not thereby destabilize the notion of racial difference itself?

The broad circulation of body parts, for Lee, displaces traditional models of both physiological racial difference and social construction theory. Lee posits that ideas of race as essential bodily divergence, and the correspondingly strict social-constructionist approaches dominant in Asian American studies, which assiduously avoid any aspect of identity correlated to biological existence (conceived as brute and limiting matter), have lost their explanatory purchase. She emphasizes the need for new analyses of race that see "biological personhood not as fixed or singular but as multiform and distributed" (15). Asian American literature and performance undertake this project, she argues, although its critics tend to elide these contributions. For instance, in Cheng-Chieh Yu's dance piece *My Father's Teeth in My Mother's Mouth*, Lee sees Yu's staging of orthodontia as suggesting the bodily regimes of biopolitics, including both the movement of labor across borders and mandates to health that demand the rearrangement of parts within the body. Throughout, Lee is careful to insist that the disintegration of the body does not usher in a postracial epoch. More likely, the fragmented body "creates micro-scale risk factors as the new markers of difference" as well as associates these factors with "anatomical markers read off the body's surface," thereby updating, rather than displacing, older frameworks of race and gender (57). This is a strong argument, particularly because the racialized body has long been understood to be fragmented and consumable.

Lee's emphasis on the circuits of bodily tissues at the level of the cell and microbe enables an expanded notion of queer reproduction and kinship. Bringing the work of feminist science studies scholars such as Myra Hird into critical race theory, Lee conceives of reproduction as the augmentation of the quantity of cells, rather than the union of male and female gametes. This enables Lee to explore how the traffic in microbes and tissue cultures lies at the intersections of race, gender, and sexuality. She identifies the "*zoe*-fication" of human lives as "a race or 'species-being' apart," a biopolitical tactic of carving up the population into the expendable bare life of animals or microbes and those whose lives this raw biological material will be used to enhance (48). She challenges this function of modern biotechnology by thinking with Yu's dance performances, Margaret Cho's comedy, Amitav Ghosh's novel *The Calcutta Chromosome*, and the theater artist Denise Uyehara, all of whom embrace the very instability of modern personhood. For these artists, Lee proposes, the entanglement of human parts and lives with other forms of life on earth works as a way to challenge traditional humanism, instead envisioning the human as "an ecology of networked plant-machine-protocist-and-animal symbionts" (49). The book draws on a wide range of theoretical, ontological, and political fields, including disability studies, Lynn Margulis's microbiology, Elizabeth Wilson's "gut feminism," histories of reproductive control, pluripotent stem cells, sentimentalism, bioethics, and affect theory. The result is more suggestive than synthetic, as the book's organization is overburdened by the weight of its multiple interpretive frames; still, Lee's study opens numerous avenues for other scholars to build on. For Lee, identifying the subindividual level of biopower opens up new pathways for resistance that transform bodily disintegration into innovative associations.

Read alongside *Testo Junkie* and *Racial Indigestion*, the contemporary market in tissue cultures, organs, and other "human fragments" on which Lee focuses constitutes less a sea change in practices of embodiment than the full flowering of a much longer tradition. Bringing Foucauldian biopower up to the conditions of the present, Preciado proposes a new regime within Western sexuality that overlaps and supersedes the disciplinary biopower characteristic of the nineteenth century: pharmacopornographic power. In *Testo Junkie*, contemporary biopower works through the "miniaturization" of control that materializes the body itself via the flow of hormones, neurotransmitters, silicone, and other pharmaceutical molecules (79). The products of "a new kind of hot, psychotropic, punk capitalism" take shape as "soft, featherweight, viscous, gelatinous technologies that can be injected, inhaled—'incorporated,'" Preciado writes (33, 77). Pharmacopornographic power emerged as the result of the postwar convergence of the chemical revolution, the medical invention of gender, the sexual revolution, and the rise of global media.

The principal engine of the contemporary economy is not finance and other imma-
terial and "chaste" labor, as other critics of neoliberalism have proposed, but the
body's capacity for excitement, its *"potentia gaudendii* or 'orgasmic force'" (70,
41). Capitalism depends on extracting the body's erotic force to produce corporate
profits, new generations, and individual subjectivity—not only as consumers, but
as *genders.*

Whereas for Lee, the micro-bioeconomy poses central questions about
the meaning of race and racialized gender, for Preciado, the excitations circulating throughout the economy produce the gendered and sexualized body. Drawing on the work of Foucault, Gilles Deleuze, Félix Guattari, Judith Butler, and
Gayle Rubin, Preciado describes how the "sex-gender" model emerged in the
mid-twentieth century and replaced the two-sex model of the disciplinary era.
Sex-gender materialized within the new role of pornography in popular culture,
the separation of heterosexuality and reproduction enabled by the pill, the invention of gender "as clinical tool," and the sciences of endocrinology, sexology, and
psychology (81). While decades of feminist theorists have embraced the notion of
gender as a strategy for illuminating how sexual difference comes to signify within
social structures, Preciado insists that "gender is a biotech industrial artifact," not
a category of liberation, and renames gender as "techno-gender" (101). He does
so through tracing the use of the term *gender* in a behavioral, rather than strictly
linguistic, sense, back to its origins in the lab of John Money and the experiments
leading to the birth control pill. This is a major contribution to feminist theory,
which has been saddled with a curious unwillingness to historicize one of its principal terms, leaving it largely reliant on an outdated biology versus culture dyad.
In *Testo Junkie*, exogenous estrogen molecules circulate throughout most bodies,
not only for deliberate (or unwilling, as in Turing's case) gender transition, but for
menstrual regulation and birth control (229). Preciado thus names cisfemininity a
form of "biodrag," a gendered subjectivity produced by the flow of pharmaceutical
molecules and media images (191).

Preciado intersperses his sweeping, synthetic theory of contemporary
power, capital, sex, and subjectivity with intimate autobiographical chapters
detailing his own experiment with testosterone and the steamy beginnings of his
relationship with the French writer Virginie Despentes. The cumulative effect is
performative manifesto, rather than traditional academic theory—we witness the
molecular flow of hormones and secretions materialize as his gendered self and
his sexuality. It is an impressive feat, if an often over-the-top paean to his erotic
prowess. Yet given the book's provocative ambition—particularly its penchant for
coining new terms—its unwillingness to conceptualize racial difference as a fun-

damental strategy of biopower reads less as a matter of manageable scope and more as a refusal to engage with some of the most important work on biopolitics, and feminism, today. Rather than engage racialization directly as a key tactic of population management, one that structures the operation of gender and sexuality and vice versa, Preciado conceptualizes race as a discrete add-on, a factor that further victimizes some in the larger scheme he calls the "pornification of work," or the harnessing of "orgasmic force" by capital (296). At its worst, the text goes so far as to echo Octavio Paz's infamous characterization of Mexicans as "la chingada," portraying the peoples of the global south as "global anuses," made supine by sexualized capitalism (303). This narrowing of biopower to the fundamental question of gender, at the exclusion of race as a structuring technology of gender itself, also limits Preciado's chosen resistance to pharmacopornpower— bodily modification, especially drag. If bodily modification is a privileged technique of resistance, does this extend to racialized subjectivity as well, and if so, what would that look like?

Preciado writes that "in the pharmacopornographic era, the body swallows power," a mode of bodily incorporation he sees as markedly different from the external architectures of nineteenth-century biopower that surrounded the individual (207). In contrast, for Tompkins, an Americanist cultural studies scholar, biopower has long depended on bodies that ingest power. Tompkins tracks the circulation of morsels of food and racialized bodies figured as food to argue that eating is itself a biopolitical practice of long standing. She illuminates "eating as a trope and technology of racial formation" through studies of nineteenth-century material culture, including novels, poetry, cookbooks, and trade cards (2). As Tompkins shows, in the nineteenth century the body came to be understood to be a porous entity with several key apertures through which matter flows in and out; eating became a biopolitical practice regulating the individual's relationship with the environment beyond its flesh. The literary, reform, and advertising texts that she considers position the mouth as the door to the body, a body that metonymizes both the domestic household and the larger nation. She uses scholarship on biopower (Foucault's *History of Sexuality*, the work of Ann Laura Stoler), affect, and performance studies to analyze racial formation as a relational process that consolidates in the interactions of material objects, individuals, and the nation. Tompkins's framing of what "counts" as food and politics emerges in the book's strongest chapter, which tracks how William Alcott and Sylvester Graham's dietary reforms materialize both the body and the imperial nation's expanding borders by categorizing healthful and dangerous foods on the basis of civilizationist paradigms. In

nineteenth-century food cultures, the regulation of the appetites of the mouth consolidates the gendered and racialized body, the emergent site of political power.

Yet one of the white mouth's key desires is revealed to be the bodies of
black subjects, who are analogized to food. Dominant-eating cultures identify the
black body as what is ingested, as bare materiality, which is threatening on its own
but, when consumed, consolidates white political subjects. For Tompkins, eating is
wrapped up in the "libidinal logic of American racism," in which the black body
functions as raw resource not only for slavery but also for some of its oppositional
discourses (90). For example, the sentimental mode in which Harriet Beecher
Stowe, Harriet E. Wilson, and others imagine the feelings of the slave relies on a
logic of consumption in which "to empathize with the slave is to internalize her,"
swallowing the other whole (113). Tompkins considers the class and sexual dimensions of this conflation, which also open possibilities for resistance when the black
body "will not go down easily," sticking in the throat even in the work of Stowe and
Nathaniel Hawthorne (11). The antebellum black cook is, on the one hand, sent
below the stairs in the kitchen, an area of domestic architecture newly separated
from the warming hearth upstairs, yet, on the other, is in control of all the food that
will pass through the household's bodies. Furthermore, the imagined ingestion of
the black body in works by Hawthorne, Stowe, and widely circulated trade cards
works through a structure of objectification that is inextricable from sexual desire.
Eating, for Tompkins, binds sexual desire to the reproduction of the race and
nation. Illuminating the "erotic and political life of the mouth," eating emerges
as a juncture between the individual and what we might call force, figured in this
period as both food and the vital elements of the black body (55).

The mouth's porosity, its role as the aperture of body, home, and nation,
renders eating an erotic practice. What Tompkins terms "queer alimentarity"
marks how the mouth functions as a key site of sex before sexuality, an intensification of the body later discarded when official sexual discourse at the turn of the
twentieth century settled solely on the genitalia. Tompkins excavates the complex
process in which oral eroticism informs dietary techniques of the self, including
white feminist projects like Louisa May Alcott's, in which food serves as an instrument of female independence. This frame enables Tompkins to effectively counter
familiar portrayals of food as merely *allegorizing* power relations, instead illuminating how the eroticized mouth (re)produces the divisions at the heart of biopower into the eaters and the eaten, a process in which racialization and desire are
interdependent. The book's analysis of biopower centers on the anatomo-politics of
individual discipline, however. Given eating's location within the gradual deploy-

ment of sexuality, a phenomenon that for Foucault came to prominence because it coordinated both the governance of the individual and the management of the population, one wonders: how did eating also function as a regulatory apparatus at the emergent biopolitical level of the population-as-species?

Tompkins's book, along with Lee's and Preciado's, makes a strong case that recent queer scholarship on biopower fundamentally shifts our analyses of not only what counts as power but what pertains to the domain of the biological. Power in these texts materializes in the form of force that circulates and aggregates below and before the level of the individual. Power transpires through a field of the consumable, penetrant, dispersible, and absorbable, coordinating life well beyond the human, beyond the nominally alive, even as it forms the shifting parameters of embodied difference. Together, this scholarship articulates a worthy challenge for the field: how to attend to the flow to force as it accumulates as race, gender, *and* sexuality, and subtends the regulation and optimization of individuals *and* populations.

Notes

1. Thanks to Greta LaFleur for thinking through *The Imitation Game* with me.
2. See also Garlick 2014.
3. See also Vora 2015.

References

Copeland, B. Jack. 2014. *Turing: Pioneer of the Information Age*. New York: Oxford University Press.

Garlick, Steve. 2014. "The Biopolitics of Masturbation: Masculinity, Complexity, and Security." *Body & Society* 22, no. 2: 44–67. bod.sagepub.com/content/early/2013 /08/08/1357034X13506945.

The Imitation Game. 2014. DVD. Directed by Morten Tyldum. Beverly Hills, CA: Anchor Bay Entertainment.

Vora, Kalindi. 2015. *Life Support: Biocapital and the New History of Outsourced Labor* Minneapolis: University of Minnesota Press.

BEYOND THE WOUND

Black Feminist Pleasure in Hard-Core Pornography

Jennifer DeClue

The Black Body in Ecstasy: Reading Race, Reading Pornography
Jennifer C. Nash
Durham, NC: Duke University Press, 2014. x + 219 pp.

Historically, black feminist epistemological frameworks have contended with psychic and corporeal wounds inflicted on black womanhood that permeate visual culture through predatory gazes and lascivious narratives. With *The Black Body in Ecstasy*, Jennifer C. Nash resists the impulse to heal wounds or protect black women in the sexual imaginary as she fearlessly explores racial-sexual taboos that tread on familiar and hyperbolic racial tropes in hard-core pornography. In its excavation of a theoretical and cinematic archive of black women's fraught relationship with pleasure, *The Black Body in Ecstasy* levies a critique of black feminism's categorical condemnation of the representation of black women in pornography without abandoning black feminist methodologies or the archive of black feminist theory. Nash's measured analysis of black women in pornography roots itself in a black feminist tradition, as it joins Mireille Miller-Young's *Taste for Brown Sugar: Black Women in Pornography* (2014) and Amber Musser's *Sensational Flesh: Race, Power, and Masochism* (2014) in ushering the field into provocative new territory.

 The Black Body in Ecstasy forwards a historical yet boundary-pushing examination of racialized pornography, a term that Nash describes as "hard-core moving-image pornography featuring black women" (2). Nash makes an intervention into black feminist analyses of black women in pornography by cultivating a theory of ecstasy that subverts injury. Through the reading practice that Nash calls *racial iconography*, she moves beyond the framework of exploitation that has dominated discussions of black women in pornography, in order to foreground often-overlooked moments of black women's sexual pleasure. Nash's conception of ecstasy does not ignore the racialization of black women's sexuality but describes ecstasy as an uneasy bliss that arises through the bodies of black women who are positioned as the object of the gaze, who relish in the thrill of performance, and who are viewers of racialized pornography.

The Black Body in Ecstasy opens with a brief yet detailed genealogy of feminist critiques and theorizations of pornography beginning with the antiporn/ proporn debates of the 1980s, followed by the sex radical position, and ending with feminist porn studies scholarship. As is characteristic of her generous methodology, Nash incorporates into her complex black feminist framework what is habitable about these feminist engagements with pornography instead of discarding them entirely because they have overlooked race or, in their engagement with race, have problematically reinforced racial difference. Nash makes two significant epistemological contributions to black feminist thought on pornography. First, by refusing to hold fast to the understanding that black women's sexual bodies are perpetually hypervisible in visual culture, Nash attends to the sustained absences of black women in the vast lexicon of hard-core porn. Second, Nash makes a dynamic revelation with implications for all of visual culture—black women's performances of racialized narratives in sexually explicit films lay bare the knowledge that "race is a pornographic fantasy" (6).

The first chapter collects an archive of black feminist theories that contend with the politics of representation, sexually explicit imagery, racialized gendered violence, and the project of recovering black women's sexual bodies from a legacy of injury. Nash's discussion of black feminist theory centers Saartjie Baartman, the Hottentot Venus, as the quintessential black female exploited body. The archive of black feminist thought that Nash assembles is accompanied by contemporary fine art photography that riffs on and reworks the image of the Hottentot Venus, providing a gentle entry into the close readings of hard-core porn that follow. Nash's vivid descriptions, replete with evocative film stills, consider the historical context and sociality implied within the narratives, performances, and visual language of the films discussed.

The second chapter looks closely at the pleasure experienced by black women performers in the 1970s golden age genre of "blax-porn-tation" (64) films, whose narrative thrust depends on a hypermasculine worship of the black phallus. Chapter 3 discusses black women's sensual power in scenes that achieve their sexual charge through the interracial taboo of black-white couplings. Though these films contain only a touch of homoerotic tension and an obligatory lesbian love scene, Nash deftly draws from queer theory to examine the pleasure achieved through racial abjection and gender performativity while considering what is productive about the performance of race and accounting for ways that sexual desire hinges on racialization. By focusing on black women's performances of seduction and arousal, Nash demonstrates these films' narrative and climactic reliance on black women's pleasure.

Nash's reading of black women protagonists in 1980's silver age porn films, offered in chapters 4 and 5, asserts that hyperbolic racial humor and taboo familial sexual encounters expose racial fictions and engender an ecstatic release by destabilizing racial hierarchies, or conversely by refusing to visualize racialized sexual difference at all. In her analysis of porn spectatorship that shifted from public theaters to private homes with the advent of the VCR, Nash demands recognition of black woman viewers of hard-core pornography who engage in the complicated labor of assimilating, discarding, and repurposing sexually explicit imagery within a rich and tailored fantasy landscape.

The Black Body in Ecstasy stretches black feminist archives of pain beyond narratives of excess and deviance, enabling black feminism to embrace black women's sexual desire within the visual field without shame and without apology. Though Nash's study of racialized pornography could have benefited from attention paid to black queer women's sexual expression, her nesting of pleasure and pain within the rubric of ecstasy has the potential to propel emerging black queer studies scholarship of sensual visual culture. *The Black Body in Ecstasy* poses a fresh set of questions as it forwards a groundbreaking black feminist approach to contending with representations of black women's ecstatic corporeality. Nash's treatment of black women's participation in hard-core pornography moves black feminism beyond the wound into the domain of ecstasy.

Jennifer DeClue is assistant professor in the Program for the Study of Women and Gender at Smith College.

References

Miller-Young, Mireille. 2014. *A Taste for Brown Sugar: Black Women in Pornography.* Durham, NC: Duke University Press.

Musser, Amber. 2014. *Sensational Flesh: Race, Power, and Masochism.* New York: New York University Press.

DOI 10.1215/10642684-3603138

NARRATING SENSATION BEFORE SUBJECTIVITY

William Hughes

Senses of the Subject
Judith Butler
New York: Fordham University Press, 2015. viii + 217 pp.

Judith Butler's *Senses of the Subject* is a collection of essays written over two decades that addresses the problem of the sensuous and affective limit that precedes the formation of the self. Here, Butler is concerned with the networks of sensation and the trajectories of affect that preexist the subject's capacity to say "I," as well as the methodological and ethical problems this presubjective state poses.

For Butler, in order for one to say "I," one must already have been affected in some way, and, in fact, being affected is part of what brings about the capacity to give an account of oneself. Because language has a retroactive temporality, any account of what has happened prior to the inception of language and the formation of a conscious "I" will arrive too late. In attempting to account for this presubjective "origin," one could certainly argue that the subject in question reconstitutes it as a fantasy, and when this happens, what is really described is the fantasy and not the preconscious conditions of being affected. Butler's answer to this objection is that we "accept this belatedness and proceed in a narrative fashion that marks the paradoxical condition of trying to relate something about my formation that is prior to my own narrative capacity and that, in fact, brings that narrative capacity about" (2). Using language to give an account of presubjective affect might be said to be "impossible," but this does not mean we cannot do it. It just means we must find the right method. For Butler, that method is narrative.

Paradoxically, a self cannot consent to be affected prior to its emergence as a self. And yet, the self can emerge only after it has been affected by the world in "radically involuntary" ways (7). This means that all subjectivity is the result of manifold, unwilled, and paradoxical processes that are simultaneously constitutive. Butler also makes it clear that a subject can break with this "matrix of relations" that instituted her subjectivity, and Butler uses the term "disorientation" to describe this breakage (9). Disorientation can sometimes be brought about by the agency of a subject, but Butler goes on to ask whether these breaks might be built into the matrix of relations that constitute us. She argues that this matrix may be said to have "a pattern of breakage" within it, suggesting that we can be broken or undone by the very relations that formed us (ibid.).

The book is composed of seven chapters and an introduction. Each chapter focuses on a different problem and set of thinkers and texts. For example, in the first chapter, on René Descartes, Butler offers a response to critics of constructionism who claim that constructionists reduce the body to being "all a matter of language" (17). Butler wants to show not simply that the body is constructed through language but that it is deconstructed through language. It is given through language, but never fully given. In Descartes she finds the spectral return of the hands and body that he seeks to deny; his body is undone through language, but because language and embodied sensation can never be separated once and for all, the body returns in the very words that disavow it.

While the chapter on Maurice Merleau-Ponty and the speculative and theological philosopher Nicolas Malebranche explores how touch inaugurates subjectivity through "a touch that belongs to no subject" (37), the chapter on Baruch Spinoza's *Ethics* is the most sustained engagement with the ethical consequences of the relationship between sensation, affect, and subjectivity that Butler describes. In the chapter, she finds a prefiguration of the death drive in Spinoza's thought and demonstrates that there is room for communal subjectivity in Spinoza's ethical framework, as opposed to the singular individualism with which he is often associated.

These first three chapters establish the argument of the collection, and the remaining four chapters elaborate on these claims in provoking ways. Butler discusses particular emotions, including love and despair, in her fourth and fifth chapters on G. W. F. Hegel and Søren Kierkegaard, respectively. In a chapter on Luce Irigaray and Merleau-Ponty, Butler reads Irigaray as enacting "relations of flesh" through her citations of Merleau-Ponty (150). The final chapter reads Frantz Fanon's *The Wretched of the Earth* alongside the preface Jean-Paul Sartre wrote for it. In these two texts, Butler identifies a logic that connects the universal masculine mode of address with a version of the human that is inaugurated by violence. However, she also identifies an alternative mode of address in the second person: the pronoun "you" opens up the possibility for a new future of the human formed through a touch other than violence.

One aspect of the argument I wanted to hear more about was on whether thinking may be said to precede subject formation. Butler is agnostic about this question, though she raises it quite early, but *Senses of the Subject* raises more questions than it attempts to answer about this possibility, which may be the stuff of another book. For her purposes here, she says that she is "not sure whether there are certain kinds of 'thoughts' that operate in the course of sensing something" (2). Instead, the argument focuses on the methodological and ethical consequences of taking the priority of the senses seriously without simply dismissing the question of presubjective thought as unimportant.

Senses of the Subject is a welcome contribution to the study of subjectivity, sensation, and affect, and will be essential reading for those working in affect theory, queer theory, feminist theory, continental philosophy, and critical theory more generally. The book asks us to use a narrative method to make sense of the conditions that preexist us while registering the ethical possibilities that method makes available, urging us toward a new future of the human.

William Hughes is a PhD candidate in the Department of English at the University of California, Davis.

DOI 10.1215/10642684-3603150

AKIN TO SEX

Durba Mitra

Given to the Goddess: South Indian Devadasis and the Sexuality of Religion
Lucinda Ramberg
Durham, NC: Duke University Press, 2014. xiv + 282 pp.

Perhaps much to the dismay of some social scientists who seek to define it, social stigma often carries no definitive markings for those who experience it. How then do we write about stigma? As Lucinda Ramberg demonstrates in her sophisticated study of the lifeworlds of devadasis in South India, *Given to the Goddess*, studying stigma requires that we revisit what counts as kinship in our everyday lives. Ramberg's ethnography explores the people who are bound in marriage to the goddess Yellamma in the Karnataka and Maharashtra regions of southern India. They are often called *devadasi* (lit., *dasi*, or "slave," to the *deva*, or "god"), or *jogati* (lit., devotees to the path). Given in marriage in devotion to the goddess, they are most often people sexed female, gendered in positions as girls and women. However, children sexed male sometimes are devoted to the goddess as well, sometimes gendered as girls, sometimes as boys. Jogati come from Dalit or outcaste communities.

Ramberg tells a story not of marginalization and recuperation, or what Anjali Arondekar (2015: 100) has cautioned against as a simplistic "telos of loss and recovery," but one of inhabitation. Stigmatization and reform appear but do not define the lifeworlds of these devotees. In this world, rituals of care for the goddess and her temple are vital, even as jogati are vilified in campaigns that promote narrow notions of a purified Hindu "religion" based in upper-caste practices. Ramberg describes the kinds of sexual labor many jogati perform in institutions of brothels and in other transactional forms. Yet she does not limit the devadasi lifeworld solely to sexual labor. Rather, Ramberg's depiction of jogati is one of difficult lives, where women are independent yet destitute, revered yet marginalized in their devotion.

In part 1, "Gods," Ramberg demonstrates the extraordinary reach of Yellamma in regional cosmologies, where the goddess represents both auspiciousness and the possibility of danger. She describes how jogati understand and describe their marginalization through a cosmology that sees reform efforts against them as part of Yellamma's plan. Ramberg details how the worldview of devotees must accommodate a changing landscape of land rights, experiences of destitution, and the pressures of exorbitant debt.

Ramberg turns from jogati understandings of the world to reform movements that target devadasi practices. She builds on the scholarship of Anupama Rao (2009) in demonstrating that the reform of Dalit women reconstitutes and empowers new forms of Dalit patriarchy. The Karnataka Devadasis (Prohibition of Dedication) Act of 1982 mobilized a range of authorities to "purify" ritual practices under a rhetoric of "good" religion and the recuperation of women from the "disreputable" lifestyles. The public health rhetoric of uncleanliness is particularly significant because of its complicity in long-standing practices of caste-based violence based on ideas of Dalit uncleanliness.

In part 2, "Gifts," Ramberg examines the power of the social reform agenda within Dalit communities and the structures of kinship and property for jogati. In her study of the practice of naked worship (*bettale seve*), Ramberg describes how Dalit reform politics seek to assimilate women's bodies into new epistemologies predicated on sexual propriety and norms of public dress. From the early 1980s, devadasi practices of naked worship have been the target of Dalit reformers who seek to police and condemn women's ecstatic bodily worship and nudity in public.

The innovation for queer studies in Ramberg's study is in her detailed ethnographic treatment of kinship practices where the jogati appear as *neither* normative *nor* antinormative. Ramberg's critiques of kinship theory appear in part 3, "Trouble," where she traces how the marriage economy of devadasis allows for capital to remain with the natal family, as the jogati daughter herself keeps wealth and inherits property. This kinship structure differs from patriarchal conjugality based in heterosexual models of marriage, biological descent, and the transfer of wealth. The jogati navigate a complex social milieu where they are independent and sometimes in possession of land and capital. Yet they remain vulnerable like the poor low-caste and Dalit communities that surround them. By addressing the simultaneity of these different kinship structures, Ramberg's study of the social life of devadasis points to the "trouble" with a singular notion of kinship.

For Ramberg, "thinking sex" requires a re-turn to the critical insights of Gayle Rubin's call in "The Traffic in Women" (1975): to interrogate gendered and sexualized norms that became foundational to our scholarly understandings of kinship. As Rubin demonstrates, the objectification and exchange of women was at the heart of structuralist anthropological theories of kinship. Ramberg builds on Rubin's critique to consider how strict interpretations of theories of kinship cannot capture the complex social roles of women jogati who play the role of sons while remaining women, or devotees who are born sexed males yet occupy fluid gender identities.

Indeed, jogati kinship, where devotees are solely married to the goddess, demonstrates the need for further engagement with the formal concept of kinship and its complicity in making conjugal marriage the primary social unit in the social sciences, from the nineteenth-century ethnology of Lewis Henry Morgan to the structuralism of Claude Lévi-Strauss and beyond. Legacies of compulsory heterosexuality and conjugal marriage in foundational theories require in-depth investigation, in that they shape and, at points, limit our understandings of sexuality. In devadasi kinship, individuals are permanently outside the heterosexual conjugal arrangement, and wealth remains in the natal lineage. Ramberg's study demonstrates not only how scholarly treatment of non-Western sexualities adds to our knowledge about sexual practices of different times and places but also how we may benefit from treating them beyond their insights as localized case studies. Indeed, these investigations reveal how the broader study of queer sociality must interrogate inherited concepts like kinship instead of solely seeking out alternatives or oppositional forms through "fictive kinship," notions of unconventional families, or queer kin. We must dwell with, as *Given to the Goddess* gracefully does, the everyday experiences of devotion, exchange, and one's social relationship to another—human, nonhuman, or even goddess—that make us, quite simply, kin.

Durba Mitra is assistant professor of history at Fordham University.

References

Arondekar, Anjali. 2015. "In the Absence of Reliable Ghosts: Sexuality, Historiography, South Asia." *differences: A Journal of Feminist Studies* 25, no. 3: 98–122.

Rao, Anupama. 2009. *The Caste Question: Dalits and the Politics of Modern India.* Berkeley: University of California Press.

DOI 10.1215/10642684-3603162

THERE IS LOTS TO SEE ABOUT SODOMY

Helmut Puff

Seeing Sodomy in the Middle Ages
Robert Mills
Chicago: University of Chicago Press, 2015. xiv + 398 pp.

When I first entered the field of gay and lesbian studies in the late 1980s, remarkably few publications shed light on images of same-sex love, friendship, and sexuality from the European Middle Ages. What there was to know about sodomy—the infamous name for a variety of illicit sex acts, including homoeroticism—revolved around words (whose conceptual and social horizons medievalists debated vividly). In the meantime, thanks to studies by, among others, Alan Bray (2003), Michael Camille (1989), and Glenn Olsen (2011), the visual representations that elucidated same-sex desires in medieval times have entered markedly into our field of vision: the volume to be reviewed here lists no less than eighty-nine illustrations.

Seeing Sodomy in the Middle Ages is nothing short of splendid, and the captivating visuals are but one aspect of its many riches. Robert Mills brings close readings, historical concerns, and theoretical insights to bear on manuscript illuminations, stone capitals, friezes, frescoes, woodcuts, drawings, and marginalia from the twelfth century to 1500 (with a focus on English and French materials). While the author draws on queer modes of analysis to unravel the multiple and ever-shifting meanings of same-sex eroticism in medieval images and texts, he also engages questions pertaining to context, circulation, media, and interpretive communities. In performing this difficult yet engrossing juggling act, Mills animates the realization that every terminological tool in approaching past sexualities, whether medieval (such as *vicium sodomiticum* or *sodomia*) or modern in origin (e.g., homosexuality), comes with its own possibilities and limitations. In the interstices between the partial views offered by the respective terms of critical choice, we can indeed make out what there is to see about medieval sodomy.

Ingeniously, this study sets out with investigating the "surge of interest in the topic . . . in thirteenth-century Paris" (30), the intellectual and political center from where much of the age's discourse on sodomy emanated. However, authoritative texts rarely, if ever, limited the function of images to illustrating certain preestablished truths. In the case of the Parisian *Bibles moralisées*, or "moralized Bibles," for royal viewers (whose reading presumably was guided by spiritual advisers), the usually assumed hierarchy of texts and images was in fact reversed: illuminations took precedence over explanations from biblical sources. This is just one example among many of the multiform text-image-relations Mills urges us to consider. In every instance, the visual and the textual media discussed have one thing in common: they actualize a passage from the past for a presumed present, thereby occasioning moral or other meanings for particular audiences. As Mills makes clear, such acts of translation were neither firmly anchored nor highly constrained by an original referent, though the representations in question certainly marshaled the great prestige of the Bible or ancient authors. Translations thus emerge as the perpetual condition for engaging sodomy, both visually and textually.

Importantly, medieval "translators" took up or confronted homoeroticism as part of the "afterlife" or "survival" of antiquity (Didi-Huberman 2003). They brought to life pertinent narratives from Ovid's *Metamorphoses*, for instance. Albrecht Dürer, as well as other artists, reenvisioned figures like Orpheus—Eurydice's lover, the great bard, and the supposed ur-sodomite of Greek mythology— or Iphis, who, having been raised as a boy, fell in love with a woman, Ianthe, and whose sex the gods reassigned so the two could marry. Transgender is a further concept that Mills introduces in the context of Ovid-inspired imagery and textual reworkings. Like translation, transgender complicates some of the either-or thinking that pervades the modern terminological apparatus on sexual matters. What if we expanded the conventional notion of sexual object choice—often said not to have existed before the rise of sexology in the nineteenth century—to include monks and nuns, Mills asks provocatively in one chapter. After all, monastics turned to or were supposed to orient their erotic desires toward God: virginity, chastity, and celibacy, he argues, may thus have been "analogous, in certain respects, to sexual orientation" (246)—an "anachronism" both risqué and revealing (247).

As has perhaps become evident in the above, the book's title is something of a pun. It conjures up a corpus of images as well as the titular term's elusive meanings. In sum, sodomy was not so "utterly confused" a category as to defy visualization (to cite Michel Foucault's [1978: 1, 101] iconic statement). Sodomy often became visually recognizable, even though few, if any, iconographical standards seem to have shaped the renderings of male-male or, rarely, female-female erotic bonds. Yet "visibility offers no easy corrective to the problem of invisibility; seeing sodomy does not necessarily generate straightforward acts of looking," Mills theorizes cunningly (13–14). This is so, among other reasons, because sodomy consistently attracted polymorphous registers of signification in addition to the sexual, including gender, religion, and ethnicity.

That Mills as a scholar stands on the shoulders of previous critics (to invoke a famous image from the Middle Ages about the era's relation to the golden standard of ancient times) without the resulting monograph neatly fitting into one discipline amounts to a veritable strength: *Seeing Sodomy in the Middle Ages* is a milestone in the historiography on sexuality, queer studies, and medievalism, and in the history of art—for all interested readers to see for themselves.

Helmut Puff is professor of German, history, and women's studies at the University of Michigan, Ann Arbor.

References

Bray, Alan. 2003. *The Friend*. Chicago: University of Chicago Press.
Camille, Michael. 1989. *The Gothic Idol: Ideology and Image-Making in Medieval Art*. Cambridge: Cambridge University Press.

Didi-Huberman, Georges. 2003. "Artistic Survival: Panofsky vs. Warburg and the Exorcism of Impure Time." *Common Knowledge* 9, no. 2: 273–85.

Foucault, Michel. (1976) 1978. *The History of Sexuality*, vol. 1: *An Introduction*. Trans. Robert Hurley. New York: Pantheon.

Olsen, Glenn W. 2011. *Of Sodomites, Effeminates, Hermaphrodites, and Androgynes: Sodomy in the Age of Peter Damian*. Toronto: Pontifical Institute of Medieval Studies.

DOI 10.1215/10642684-3603174

About the Contributors

Paul Amar is a professor in the Global Studies program at the University of California, Santa Barbara. His books include *Cairo Cosmopolitan: Politics, Culture and Urban Space in the New Middle East* (2006), *New Racial Missions of Policing: International Perspectives on Evolving Law-Enforcement Politic* (2010), *Global South to the Rescue: Emerging Humanitarian Superpowers and Globalizing Rescue Industries* (2011), *Dispatches from the Arab Spring: Understanding the New Middle East* (2013), and *The Middle East and Brazil: Perspectives on the New Global South* (2014). His book *The Security Archipelago: Human-Security States, Sexuality Politics, and the End of Neoliberalism* was awarded the Charles Taylor Book Award for the best political science book in 2014 by the Interpretive Methods Section of the American Political Science Association.

Julian Gill-Peterson is assistant professor of English and children's literature at the University of Pittsburgh. He is currently at work on a book on the transgender child across the twentieth century. His work has also appeared in *Women and Performance* (2015), *WSQ: Women's Studies Quarterly* (2015), *Transgender Studies Quarterly* (2014), and *GLQ* (2013).

Clifford Rosky is professor of law at the University of Utah. He is a two-time recipient of the Dukeminier Award, which recognizes the best legal scholarship on sexual orientation and gender identity published in the previous year. His research on childhood, queerness, and the LGBT movement has been published in numerous law reviews and anthologies, including the *Yale Journal of Law & Feminism*, the *Cardozo Law Review*, the *Journal of Sex Research*, and *After Marriage Equality: The Future of LGBT Rights* (2016).

Kyla Schuller is assistant professor of women's and gender studies at Rutgers University, New Brunswick, where she teaches and researches the intersections between race, gender, sexuality, and the sciences. Her first book, *The Biopolitics of Feeling*, is forthcoming from Duke University Press. Her work has appeared in *American Quarterly, Discourse, Journal of Modern Literature*, and other venues.

Rebekah Sheldon is assistant professor of English at Indiana University Bloomington. She is the author of *The Child to Come: Life after the Human Catastrope*, which is forthcoming from the University of Minnesota Press in 2016. Her essays on feminist science fiction, feminist science studies, and queer theories of the child have appeared in *Science Fiction Studies* and *Ada: Journal of Gender, New Media, and Technology* as well as in the edited collections *The Nonhuman Turn* and *The Cambridge Companion to American Science Fiction*.

Kathryn Bond Stockton is distinguished professor of English and associate vice president for equity and diversity at the University of Utah. Her most recent books, *Beautiful Bottom, Beautiful Shame: Where "Black" Meets "Queer"* (2006) and *The Queer Child, or Growing Sideways in the Twentieth Century* (2009), are published by Duke University Press and both were finalists for the Lambda Literary Award in LGBT Studies.

Mary Zaborskis is a doctoral candidate in English at the University of Pennsylvania. Her dissertation examines the management of childhood sexuality in North American boarding schools established for marginalized populations in the nineteenth and twentieth centuries. Her work has appeared in *WSQ: Women's Studies Quarterly*, *Journal of Homosexuality*, and *Public Books*.

DOI 10.1215/10642684-3713480

Gender and Sexuality

ZED

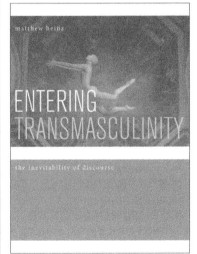

⊕ intellect

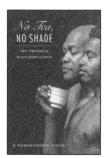

Printed and bound by CPI Group (UK) Ltd, Croydon, CR0 4YY

13/04/2025

14656485-0003